100 delicious Biscuits and Suces

Souvenir Press

Contents

How to Bake Beautiful Biscuits —————————————————————5
Everyday Biscuits —————————————————————————————6
Cereal Biscuits —————————————————————————————8
Coconut Biscuits —————————————————————————————10
Nut Biscuits —————————————————————————————12
Ginger Biscuits —————————————————————————————13
Honey Biscuits —————————————————————————————14
Meringues and Macaroons —————————————————————————16
Favourite Biscuits —————————————————————————————18
Shortbread —————————————————————————————22
Savoury Biscuits —————————————————————————————24
Old Fashioned Favourites —————————————————————————26
Health Biscuits —————————————————————————————28
International Biscuits —————————————————————————————30
No-Bake Biscuits —————————————————————————————32
Special Occasion Biscuits —————————————————————————34
Slices —————————————————————————————38
Index —————————————————————————————45

Oven Temperatures

Electric Temperatures

	Fahrenheit	Celsius
Very slow	250	120
Slow	300	150
Moderately slow	325–350	160–180
Moderate	375–400	190–200
Moderately hot	425–450	220–230
Hot	475–500	250–260
Very hot	525–550	270–290

Gas Temperatures

	Fahrenheit	Celsius
Very slow	250	120
Slow	275–300	140–150
Moderately slow	325	160
Moderate	350	180
Moderately hot	375	190
Hot	400–450	200–230
Very hot	475–500	250–260

Cup Measures

	Metric	Imperial
1 cup flour	125 g	$4\frac{1}{2}$ oz.
1 cup sugar (crystal or castor)	250 g	8 oz.
1 cup brown sugar, firmly packed	185 g	6 oz.
1 cup icing sugar, sifted	185 g	6 oz.
1 cup shortening (butter, margarine, etc.)	250 g	8 oz.
1 cup honey, golden syrup, treacle	375 g	12 oz.
1 cup fresh breadcrumbs	60 g	2 oz.
1 cup packet dry breadcrumbs	155 g	5 oz.
1 cup crushed biscuit crumbs	125 g	4 oz.
1 cup rice, uncooked	220 g	7 oz.
1 cup mixed fruit or individual fruit such as sultanas, etc.	185 g	6 oz.
1 cup nuts, chopped	125 g	4 oz.
1 cup coconut, desiccated	90 g	3 oz.

Liquid Measures

(Using the eight-liquid-ounce cup measure)

1 cup liquid	8 oz.
$2\frac{1}{2}$ cups liquid	20 oz. (1 pint)
1 gill liquid	5 oz. ($\frac{1}{4}$ pint)

How to bake beautiful biscuits

Points to remember when mixing:

1. Do not over-cream butter and sugar mixtures. Beat the butter until smooth, add sugar all at once, beat only until combined. Add beaten egg gradually, beat only until combined. Over-creaming will give a too-soft mixture which could cause biscuits to spread excessively.

2. Add sifted dry ingredients in two lots for easier mixing.

Type of tin

It is important that the correct tin be used for baking biscuits, to ensure even baking and browning. Use flat aluminium tin, which has little or no sides, such as a scone or oven tray. If the sides are more than $\frac{1}{2}$ in. high, the heat cannot circulate around the biscuits; they do not brown evenly.

Preparation of tin

Use a pastry brush to brush tin evenly and lightly with melted butter. Too-heavy greasing could cause biscuits to over-brown on base.

Baking

Several trays of biscuits can be baked in the oven at the same time, providing the trays do not touch the oven sides, or oven door when it is closed. There must be at least 1 in. space around each tray to allow the heat to circulate and brown biscuits evenly. To allow even baking, alternate the trays in the oven after half the baking time has expired.

Oven Positions

In gas oven: top half of a gas oven is best for biscuits.

In electric oven: lower half of oven is best for biscuits.

To test if biscuits are cooked

Biscuits generally feel soft in the oven and become firmer when cold. (If biscuits are very soft when cooked, loosen with knife or spatula, and lift on to wire rack to cool. Some of the more crisp type of biscuits are cooled on the oven trays. Individual recipes state when it is necessary to cool on trays.)

A good test for most types of biscuits baked on trays is to push a biscuit on the tray gently with the finger; if it can be moved, without breaking, the biscuits are cooked.

Some faults that may occur when baking biscuits

If recipes in this book are followed according to directions, perfect biscuits will result. However, for interest, we set out some of the more common faults that occur when baking biscuits.

If biscuits spread on tray: the mixture is too soft, due to over-creaming; incorrect measuring of ingredients; incorrect flour has been used (such as self-raising when the recipe calls for plain flour); or oven was not hot enough to set mixture quickly.

If biscuits are too hard: ingredients have been measured incorrectly, or biscuits have been baked too long, or at too high a temperature, or incorrect types of oven trays have been used.

If biscuits are too soft: they have not been cooked long enough, or they have been stacked on top of each other to cool after baking. Most biscuits should have air circulating around them to crisp. Most biscuits should be left on oven trays for a few minutes after removing from oven (if moved too quickly, they could break, or their shape would be spoilt); they are then transferred to wire racks to cool so that steam can escape.

If biscuits are too brown underneath: too much greasing has probably been used; excess greasing quickly attracts heat to base of biscuit. Incorrect oven position and temperature could also be the cause. If baking two trays of biscuits at a time, it is important for even browning to reverse trays in the oven half way through baking time. Excess sweetening, such as sugar, honey or golden syrup etc. in a biscuit will also cause excessive browning.

Storage

Store in air-tight container. Biscuits must be completely cold before storing, or they will soften. Biscuits which are filled with jam or cream, or are iced, are best eaten the same day; fillings and icings soften them. Biscuits should not be stored with cakes, bread, scones etc., as the biscuits will absorb moisture from these and will soften.

If plain biscuits do soften, they can be placed on oven trays and reheated in a moderate oven for approximately 5 minutes, to recrisp.

Everyday Biscuits

Vanilla Biscuits

1½ cups self-raising flour	1 cup sugar
½ cup plain flour	1 egg
¼ teaspoon salt	1 teaspoon vanilla
4 oz. butter	2 teaspoons milk

Sift plain flour and set aside. Sift self-raising flour and salt. Cream butter, add sugar gradually, beat until light and fluffy. Add well-beaten egg, vanilla, and milk. Add sifted dry ingredients except plain flour, then gradually work in the plain flour until dough is firm enough to handle. Refrigerate at least 1 hour.

Roll out dough to ⅛ in. thickness on lightly floured board, cut with floured 2 in. biscuit cutter. Put on lightly greased oven trays, sprinkle lightly with sugar or hundreds-and-thousands. Bake in moderate oven 8 to 10 minutes. (Biscuits can be left plain, then, when cool, topped with icing.)

Makes approx. 4 dozen.

Lemon Shortbread Biscuits

1½ cups plain flour	¼ cup icing sugar
½ cup custard powder	1 tablespoon grated
6 oz. butter	lemon rind

Cream together butter and sifted icing sugar until light and fluffy, add lemon rind. Add sifted dry ingredients, mix to a stiff dough. Roll into small balls with palms of hands. Place on ungreased oven trays, flatten with fork; dip fork in flour occasionally to prevent it sticking to dough. Bake in moderate oven 10 to 15 minutes.

Makes approximately 2½ dozen.

Date and Walnut Cookies ✓

4 oz. butter	½ cup chopped walnuts
½ cup sugar	1 tablespoon lemon juice
1 egg	2 cups self-raising flour
4 oz. dates	

Cream butter and sugar, add egg, beat well. Chop dates, fold into mixture with walnuts.

Add sifted flour and lemon juice, stir well to combine all ingredients. Drop in teaspoonfuls on to greased oven trays, flatten slightly with a floured knife.

Bake in a moderate oven for 15 minutes. Leave to cool on trays.

Makes approx. 4 dozen.

Coconut Fruit Fingers ✓

Base:

4 oz. butter	1 cup plain flour
½ cup sugar	1 cup self-raising flour
1 egg	¼ cup milk
1 teaspoon vanilla	

Filling:

2 cups currants	½ cup raspberry jam

Topping:

2 oz. butter	2 tablespoons
¼ cup sugar	self-raising flour
2 eggs	2 cups coconut
½ teaspoon vanilla	

Base: Cream butter and sugar until light and fluffy, add egg and vanilla, beat well. Sift flours and fold through mixture alternately with milk. Spread evenly over base of well-greased 12 in. x 10 in. swiss roll tin, then spread filling mixture on top. Spread topping mixture evenly over filling.

Bake in moderately hot oven for 10 minutes, reduce heat to moderate, bake a further 10 minutes. When cool, cut into fingers.

Filling: Heat jam slightly in saucepan, add currants, mix well.

Topping: Cream butter and sugar until light and fluffy, beat in eggs one at a time, add vanilla. Fold in sifted flour and coconut.

Currant Cookies

2 cups plain flour	2 teaspoons grated
5 oz. butter	lemon rind
¾ cup currants	1 egg
½ cup sugar	extra sugar

Sift flour into basin, rub in butter until mixture resembles fine breadcrumbs. Add currants, sugar and lemon rind; mix well. Add beaten egg, mix to firm dough. Roll out on lightly floured surface to ¼ in. thickness, cut into rounds with 3 in. fluted cutter. Place on lightly greased oven trays, bake in moderate oven 15 to 20 minutes, or until lightly browned. While still hot, sprinkle with extra sugar.

Makes approximately 2 dozen.

Melting Moments, see page 26.

Cereal Biscuits

Anzac Biscuits

1 cup rolled oats	2 tablespoons
¾ cup coconut	boiling water
1 cup plain flour	1 cup sugar
1½ teaspoons bicarbonate	4 oz. butter
of soda	1 tablespoon golden syrup

Combine rolled oats, sifted flour, sugar and coconut. Combine butter and golden syrup, stir over gentle heat until melted. Mix soda with boiling water, add to melted butter mixture, stir into dry ingredients. Spoon dessertspoonsful of mixture on to greased oven trays; allow room for spreading.

Bake in slow oven 20 minutes. Loosen on trays while warm, then cool on trays.

Makes approx. 3 dozen.

Easy Biscuits

3 cups rice bubbles	2 teaspoons honey
½ cup sugar	1 cup coconut
1 cup self-raising flour	2 tablespoons water
4 oz. butter	

Combine rice bubbles, sugar, coconut and sifted flour in bowl; mix well. Heat butter, honey and water, pour over dry ingredients; mix well. Put teaspoonfuls of mixture on to greased oven trays.

Bake in moderate oven 12 to 15 minutes or until golden brown. Cool on trays.

Makes approx. 3 dozen.

Lunchbox Cookies

3 oz. butter	½ teaspoon salt
½ cup brown sugar	½ teaspoon
½ cup castor sugar	ground ginger
1 teaspoon vanilla	½ teaspoon cinnamon
1 egg	1¼ cups rolled oats
1¼ cups plain flour	¼ cup marmalade
¼ cup self-raising flour	1 cup chopped raisins
½ teaspoon bicarbonate	or sultanas
of soda	

Cream butter and sugars, beat in egg and vanilla. Sift dry ingredients together, add to creamed mixture, then fold in oats, marmalade and raisins. Drop by teaspoonfuls on to greased oven trays.

Bake in moderately hot oven 15 minutes or until evenly browned.

Makes approx. 3½ dozen.

Oaty Crisps

1 cup plain flour	½ teaspoon bicarbonate
1 cup coconut	of soda
1 cup rolled oats	2 tablespoons golden syrup
¾ cup sugar	4 oz. butter

Sift flour and soda, combine with remaining dry ingredients in bowl. Combine golden syrup and butter in saucepan; heat until butter melts; stir into dry ingredients, mix thoroughly.

Roll mixture into balls the size of a walnut; put 2 in. apart on greased oven trays. Bake in slow oven 15 to 20 minutes.

Makes approx. 2 dozen.

Cornflake Biscuits

4 oz. butter	1 egg
¾ cup sugar	1 cup self-raising flour
1 cup sultanas or	cornflakes
chopped mixed fruit	

Cream butter and sugar until light and fluffy, add egg; beat well. Fold in sifted flour alternately with fruit.

Roll teaspoonfuls of mixture in lightly crushed cornflakes, put on greased oven trays, allowing room for spreading. Bake in moderate oven 10 to 15 minutes.

Makes approx. 3 dozen.

Oatmeal Crunchies

¾ cup plain flour	¼ teaspoon salt
¼ cup self-raising flour	½ teaspoon
½ cup sugar	bicarbonate soda
½ cup brown sugar	¾ cup rolled oats
4 oz. butter	¼ cup chopped walnuts
1 egg	extra sugar
¼ teaspoon vanilla	

Cream together butter and sugars until light and fluffy, add egg and vanilla, beat well. Add sifted dry ingredients, oats and nuts, blend well.

Place teaspoonfuls on ungreased oven trays, sprinkle with a little extra sugar. Bake in moderate oven 10 to 12 minutes. Leave on tray a few minutes, cool on wire rack.

Makes approx. 3½ dozen.

Lemon Cookies

2 cups self-raising flour	2 teaspoons grated
5 oz. butter	lemon rind
¾ cup sugar	2 cups rice bubbles,
2 eggs	approx.

Cream butter and sugar until light and fluffy. Add eggs and lemon rind, beat well. Fold in sifted flour; mix well. Drop teaspoonfuls of mixture into rice bubbles; roll lightly.

Place on lightly greased oven trays. Bake in a moderately hot oven 10 to 12 minutes.

Makes approx. 3½ dozen.

Nutties

2 cups rolled oats	1 cup plain flour
½ cup sugar	4 oz. butter
1 teaspoon golden	½ teaspoon bicarbonate
syrup or honey	of soda
2 tablespoons boiling water	¼ cup chopped nuts

Sift flour, add rolled oats and sugar. Melt butter in saucepan, remove from heat, add golden syrup, water and soda; stir well. Combine butter mixture with dry ingredients, add nuts, mix well; roll into small balls the size of a walnut.

Place on greased oven trays, flatten with fork. Bake in moderate oven 10 minutes. Leave on trays to cool.

Makes approx. 3 dozen.

Butter Oat Biscuits

4 oz. butter	2 cups rolled oats
½ cup castor sugar	1 teaspoon bicarbonate
2 teaspoons treacle	of soda
or golden syrup	¼ cup boiling water
1 cup self-raising flour	

Cream butter and sugar, add treacle, and cream well. Blend in sifted flour and oats. Dissolve soda in boiling water and add to mixture while still hot. Mix to a stiff dough.

Roll teaspoonfuls of mixture into balls; place on greased oven trays, allowing room for spreading; press flat with fork. Bake in moderate oven approximately 15 minutes. Cool on trays.

Makes approx. 4 dozen.

Honey Oat Biscuits

¾ cup plain flour	1½ cup rolled oats
pinch salt	⅔ cup coconut
¼ teaspoon baking powder	5 oz. butter
¾ cup sugar	1 tablespoon honey

Sift together dry ingredients, add rolled oats and coconut. Melt butter, stir in honey, add to dry ingredients, mix well.

Press firmly into well-greased swiss roll tin, approximately 12 in. x 10 in. Bake in moderate oven 15 minutes. Cut into fingers while hot. Cool on tray.

Wholemeal Oat Biscuits

½ cup wholemeal	2 oz. butter
self-raising flour	2 tablespoons golden
½ cup plain flour	syrup
1 teaspoon ground ginger	2 teaspoons water
1 teaspoon mixed spice	½ teaspoon bicarbonate
½ cup rolled oats	of soda
¼ cup brown sugar	blanched almonds
1 teaspoon grated	
lemon rind	

Sift flours and spices into basin, add oats, sugar and lemon rind; mix well. Add combined melted butter and golden syrup, then soda which has been dissolved in the water; mix well to a stiff dough. Roll mixture into balls ¾ in. in diameter, place on lightly greased oven trays, top with almond half. Bake in moderate oven 12 to 15 minutes, place on wire rack to cool.

Makes approx. 2½ dozen.

Caramel Cornflake Cookies

4 oz. butter	½ cup coconut
½ cup brown sugar,	3 cups cornflakes
lightly packed	½ cup finely chopped
½ cup castor sugar	mixed nuts

Melt butter over low heat, add sugars, stir until well combined. Add coconut, lightly crushed cornflakes and nuts; mix well. Place teaspoonfuls of mixture on to lightly greased oven trays; press mixture together with fingers. Bake in moderate oven 8 to 10 minutes, cool on wire rack.

Makes approx. 2 dozen.

Coconut Biscuits

Crisp Coconut Biscuits

4 oz. butter	pinch salt
1 cup castor sugar	1 cup coconut
1 egg	extra sugar
2 cups self-raising flour	

Cream butter and sugar, beat in egg, add sifted flour, salt and coconut. Roll into balls and press flat between the hands. Dip the top side into extra sugar.

Place on greased oven trays, allow for spreading. Bake in moderately hot oven 10 to 15 minutes.

Makes approx. 2 dozen.

Coconut Crunch Biscuits

1 egg	2 cups coconut
⅔ cup sugar	1 cup self-raising flour
2 oz. butter	

Beat together egg and sugar until thick and creamy. Add cooled, melted butter, coconut and sifted flour, mix well.

Place in heaps on ungreased oven trays. Bake in slow oven 15 minutes until pale golden colour. Leave on trays until cold.

Makes approx. 2½ dozen.

Chocolate Coconut Bars

Base:

3 oz. butter	¼ cup self-raising flour
2 tablespoons castor sugar	1 tablespoon cornflour
¾ cup plain flour	½ teaspoon vanilla

Filling:

2 cups coconut	2 tablespoons
1 egg	self-raising flour
¼ cup sugar	¾ cup milk
½ teaspoon vanilla	

Icing:

1½ cups icing sugar	1 oz. butter
2 tablespoons cocoa	1 tablespoon water

5 Crisp

Base: Cream butter and sugar, add vanilla, then sifted dry ingredients; mix well. Press mixture over base of greased 7 in. x 11 in. lamington tin. Bake in moderate oven 20 minutes.

Remove, spread evenly with coconut filling. Return to oven, bake further 25 minutes.

Remove from oven, stand 5 minutes, top with icing, cut into bars when cold.

Filling: Combine dry ingredients in basin, add combined beaten egg, milk and vanilla; mix well.

Icing: Sift icing sugar and cocoa into basin, add softened butter and water, beat until smooth.

Cherry Tops

4 oz. butter	¼ cup chopped
½ cup sugar	glacé cherries
1 egg	1 cup coconut
1¼ cups self-raising flour	2 oz. blanched almonds
	extra glacé cherries

Cream butter and sugar until light and creamy, add egg, beat well. Add sifted flour, cherries, coconut and chopped almonds, mix well.

Place teaspoonfuls of mixture on greased oven trays, top each with a small piece of glacé cherry. Bake in moderate oven 15 minutes. Leave on tray a few minutes; cool on wire rack.

Makes approx. 3½ dozen.

Orange Coconut Cookies

1½ cups self-raising flour	1 tablespoon grated
4 oz. butter	orange rind
½ cup castor sugar	1 tablespoon orange juice
½ cup coconut	extra sugar

Sift flour into basin, rub in butter, add remaining dry ingredients, mix well. Stir in orange rind and juice.

Roll mixture into balls, toss in extra sugar. Place on lightly greased oven trays, about 2 in. apart; bake in moderate oven 10 to 15 minutes.

Makes approx. 3 dozen.

Coconut Cookies ✓

14 oz. can condensed milk	2½ cups coconut
⅓ cup chopped nuts	4 oz. finely chopped dates
1 teaspoon vanilla	pinch salt

Combine all ingredients in mixing bowl, mix well. Drop teaspoonfuls on to greased oven trays, approximately 1 in. apart.

Bake in moderately slow oven 12 minutes, or until lightly golden brown.

Makes approx. 5 dozen.

Crisp Coconut Biscuits, see page 10.

Nut Biscuits

Peanut Crisps

4 oz. butter	½ teaspoon bicarbonate
1 cup sugar	of soda
1 egg	1 cup rolled oats
¾ cup plain flour	½ cup chopped
¼ cup self-raising flour	salted peanuts
pinch salt	1 cup cornflakes

Cream butter and sugar, add egg; beat well. Fold in sifted flours, salt and soda. Work in the rolled oats, peanuts and cornflakes, blend well.

Put teaspoonfuls on greased oven trays, leaving room for spreading. Bake in hot oven 10 minutes. Cool on trays.

Makes approx. 4½ dozen.

Peanut Cookies

8 oz. butter	1 cup rolled oats
1 cup brown sugar,	1 cup coconut
firmly packed	4 oz. salted peanuts
1 egg	½ cup finely crushed
1½ cups self-raising flour	cornflakes
1 teaspoon bicarbonate	extra cornflakes
of soda	

Cream butter and sugar until light and fluffy, add egg; beat well. Fold in sifted flour and soda. Add rolled oats, coconut, peanuts and cornflakes; mix well.

Put teaspoonfuls of mixture on to greased oven trays; allow room for spreading. Flatten slightly with the bottom of a glass dipped in extra crushed cornflakes. Bake in moderate oven 10 to 12 minutes or until golden brown.

Makes approx. 5 dozen.

Apricot and Nut Cookies

4 oz. butter	pinch salt
⅓ cup sugar	2 oz. chopped mixed
1 egg-yolk	nuts
½ teaspoon vanilla	apricot jam
1½ cups plain flour	

Cream together butter and sugar until light and fluffy, add egg-yolk and vanilla, beat well. Stir in sifted dry ingredients and nuts, blend well.

Shape into small balls, place on ungreased oven trays. Make a deep dent in centre of each with finger. Bake in slow oven 30 minutes. Cool on wire rack. Spoon a little jam into centres.

Makes approx. 1½ dozen.

Almond Crisps

½ cup sugar	¼ cup slivered almonds
½ cup brown sugar	¾ cup plain flour
4 oz. butter	¼ teaspoon baking powder
1 egg	pinch salt
½ teaspoon vanilla	1½ cups rolled oats

Cream together butter and sugars, add vanilla, beat until light and fluffy. Add egg, beat well. Fold in slivered almonds and flour which has been sifted with baking powder and salt; fold in rolled oats.

Place by teaspoonfuls on greased oven trays. If desired, lightly press a slice of almond on top of each biscuit. Bake in moderate oven 10 to 12 minutes.

Makes approx. 3 dozen.

Peanut Butter Biscuits

4 oz. butter	¼ cup milk
¾ cup sugar	1¾ cups self-raising
1½ tablespoons	flour
peanut butter	1 teaspoon vanilla

Cream together butter and sugar until light and fluffy, add peanut butter and vanilla, beat well. Stir in milk and sifted flour, mix well.

Roll into small balls, place on lightly greased oven trays. Press down with fork; dip fork in flour occasionally to prevent sticking. Bake in moderate oven 15 minutes.

Makes approx. 3 dozen.

Raspberry Almond Fingers

1 cup plain flour	1 teaspoon water
2 oz. ground almonds	1½ tablespoons
3 oz. butter	raspberry jam
¼ cup castor sugar	1 egg-white
1 egg-yolk	extra sugar

Sift flour into basin, add almonds, rub in butter, add sugar; mix well. Add beaten egg-yolk and water to well in centre of dry ingredients, mix to stiff dough. Place on floured surface, knead lightly until smooth. Divide dough in half, roll each half to approximately 9 in. square.

Place one square of dough on lightly greased oven trays. Make a deep dent in centre of each dough. Glaze with lightly beaten egg-white, sprinkle with extra sugar.

Bake in moderate oven 15 minutes, or until lightly browned. Trim edges neatly, cut into finger lengths while still hot, cool on wire rack.

Ginger Biscuits

Ginger Nuts

2 cups plain flour	pinch salt
1 cup castor sugar	2 teaspoons ground ginger
$\frac{1}{2}$ teaspoon bicarbonate of soda	4 oz. butter
1 teaspoon cinnamon	1 small egg
	1 teaspoon golden syrup

Sift into basin flour, sugar, soda, cinnamon, salt and ginger. Rub in butter until mixture is of very fine crumb consistency. Beat egg with golden syrup, add to dry ingredients. Work into firm dough with hands.

Roll into small balls approx. $\frac{1}{2}$ in. diameter. Put on greased oven trays, about 2 in. apart. Bake in moderately slow oven approximately 15 minutes. Loosen, cool on trays.

Makes approx. $3\frac{1}{2}$ dozen.

Preserved Ginger Biscuits

4 oz. butter	2 cups self-raising flour
$\frac{1}{4}$ cup sugar	2 oz. preserved ginger
1 egg	

Cream butter and sugar until light and fluffy. Add egg, beat well; add finely chopped ginger and sifted flour, mix well. Turn on to lightly floured surface; knead lightly.

Divide mixture in half; roll each portion into log shape, approximately 7 in. long by $1\frac{1}{2}$ in. in diameter. Wrap in greaseproof paper, freeze 1 hour or until firm.

Remove from freezer, cut into $\frac{1}{4}$ in. slices. Put on greased oven trays. Bake in moderate oven 15 to 20 minutes or until golden brown.

Makes approx. 4 dozen.

Ginger Biscuits

4 oz. butter	2 cups self-raising flour
$\frac{1}{4}$ cup golden syrup	2 teaspoons ground ginger
$\frac{1}{4}$ cup water	$\frac{3}{4}$ cup brown sugar, lightly packed
$\frac{1}{2}$ teaspoon bicarbonate of soda	

Place butter, golden syrup, water and soda in saucepan, heat gently until butter is melted. Sift dry ingredients in bowl, add butter mixture; stir well, cool.

Roll into small balls the size of a walnut, place on greased oven trays; press tops with fork. Bake in moderate oven 10 to 15 minutes.

Makes approx. 4 dozen.

Gingerbread Men

4 oz. butter	3 teaspoons ground ginger
$\frac{1}{2}$ cup sugar	$2\frac{1}{2}$ tablespoons golden syrup
1 egg-yolk	currants
$2\frac{1}{2}$ cups plain flour	coloured sweets
1 teaspoon bicarbonate of soda	

Cream butter and sugar, add egg-yolk, beat well. Gradually add sifted dry ingredients and warmed syrup; mix well; knead lightly, roll to $\frac{1}{8}$ in. thickness on lightly floured board. Cut out, using special shaped cutter, or cut round cardboard shape with pointed knife.

Place on greased oven trays; add currants to represent eyes. Bake in moderate oven 15 minutes. Allow to cool before removing from trays. Decorate with coloured sweets for buttons; secure sweets with jam or icing.

Makes approx. 2 dozen.

Ginger Currant Cookies

4 oz. butter	$1\frac{1}{4}$ cups plain flour
$\frac{3}{4}$ cup sugar	$\frac{1}{2}$ cup self-raising flour
1 egg	1 tablespoon milk
$\frac{1}{2}$ cup finely chopped preserved ginger	1 egg-white
$\frac{1}{2}$ cup currants	extra sugar

Beat butter until creamy, add sugar and egg, beat until combined; do not over-cream. Add ginger, currants, milk and half the sifted flours; stir well, add remaining sifted flours.

Roll teaspoonfuls of mixture into balls, dip top in lightly beaten egg-white, then in sugar. Place about 2 in. apart (sugar-side uppermost) on lightly greased oven trays, bake in moderate oven 20 minutes. Cool on trays 5 minutes, place on wire rack to cool completely.

Makes approx. 2 dozen.

Honey Biscuits

Honey Banana Biscuits

4 oz. butter	1 cup coconut
½ cup brown sugar	pinch nutmeg
¼ cup honey	2 cups self-raising flour
1 egg	1½ cups crushed
1 large banana	cornflakes, approx.

Cream butter, sugar and honey until light and fluffy, add egg, beat well. Add peeled, mashed banana and coconut, beat well. Fold in sifted flour and nutmeg.

Drop teaspoonfuls of mixture on to cornflakes, roll lightly to coat mixture. Place on greased oven trays, bake in moderate oven approximately 12 minutes or until light golden brown.

Makes approx. 4 dozen.

Honey-Coconut Biscuits

4 oz. butter	1½ cups self-raising flour
1 tablespoon honey	1 cup sugar
1 egg-yolk	½ cup coconut

Melt butter and honey over low heat, cool slightly, add egg-yolk; mix well. Combine sifted flour, sugar and coconut, add to butter mixture, mix until well combined.

Roll teaspoonfuls of mixture into balls, place on lightly greased oven trays, and press flat. Bake in moderate oven 10 to 12 minutes; allow to cool on trays.

Makes approx. 3½ dozen.

Honey Sultana Cookies

2 oz. butter	2 tablespoons coconut
2 tablespoons honey	1 cup lightly crushed
½ cup brown sugar,	cornflakes
lightly packed	2 cups self-raising flour
1 egg	½ teaspoon nutmeg
1 cup sultanas	

Beat butter, honey and brown sugar until combined; add egg, beat well. Add sultanas, coconut, cornflakes and sifted flour and nutmeg; mix well.

Roll teaspoonfuls of mixture into balls, place on lightly greased oven trays, bake in moderate oven 15 to 20 minutes.

Makes approx. 2 dozen.

Lemon-Honey Drops

4 oz. butter	2 tablespoons honey
¼ cup castor sugar	1 egg
1 tablespoon grated	¾ cup coconut
lemon rind	⅓ cup lemon butter
2 cups self-raising flour	

Cream butter, honey and sugar together in bowl. Add egg and lemon rind, beat well. Gradually fold in sifted flour. Drop teaspoonfuls of mixture into coconut. Roll into balls between palms of hands. Place on to greased oven trays; make a small indentation with little finger in top-centre of each biscuit. Carefully spoon small quantity of lemon butter into indentation.

Bake in moderate oven approximately 12 to 15 minutes. Cool on trays.

Makes approx. 3½ dozen.

Orange Honey Cookies

1 cup self-raising flour	1 egg
½ cup plain flour	½ cup honey
½ teaspoon salt	½ cup chopped
2 oz. butter	mixed peel
¼ cup sugar	

Cream butter and sugar, add egg, beat well. Add chopped peel and honey; fold in sifted flours and salt; combine thoroughly.

Drop teaspoonfuls on to greased oven trays, bake in moderate oven 12 to 15 minutes or until golden brown.

Makes approx. 2½ dozen.

Honey Ginger Snaps

2 oz. butter	1½ teaspoons ground
⅓ cup honey	ginger
½ cup brown sugar,	1 cup plain flour
firmly packed	

Combine butter and honey in saucepan, stir over low heat until butter is melted. Pour into well in centre of sifted dry ingredients, beat until smooth. Drop level teaspoonfuls of mixture on to greased oven trays, bake in moderate oven 5 minutes, or until golden brown. Loosen on trays, cool on trays. These biscuits will become very crisp when cold.

Makes approx. 3 dozen.

From left to right: top row, Almond and Date Meringue, Coffee Cream Meringue; second row, Walnut Meringue, Almond Rock Meringue; third row, One-egg Meringue, Brown Sugar Meringue.

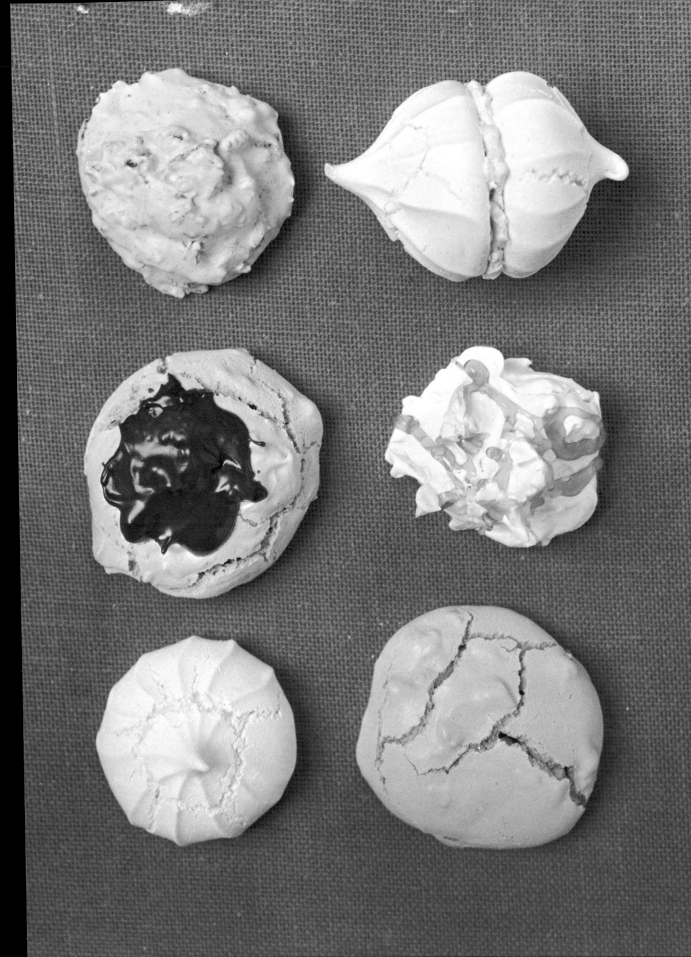

Meringues and Macaroons

Brown Sugar Meringues

3 oz. blanched almonds
2 egg-whites
1¼ cups brown sugar,
  firmly packed

½ teaspoon vanilla

Toast almonds in moderate oven until lightly browned; chop coarsely. Beat egg-whites until soft peaks form; gradually add sugar, beat until dissolved. Fold in vanilla and chopped almonds.

Drop by dessertspoonfuls on to greased and cornfloured oven trays. Bake in very slow oven 1 to 1¼ hours, or until firm to touch.

Makes approx. 1 dozen.

Almond Rock Meringues

1 cup sugar
¼ cup water
1¼ cups icing sugar

4 oz. slivered almonds
4 egg-whites

Combine sugar and water in saucepan, stir constantly over low heat until dissolved; bring to boil, boil to 250 degrees F on sweets thermometer, or until syrup forms a soft ball when a little is dropped into cold water.

Beat egg-whites until stiff, add syrup in a thin stream, beating constantly until mixture is stiff (approximately 10 minutes). Fold in sifted icing sugar and almonds.

Using piping bag with large plain tube, pipe mixture on to greased and cornfloured trays. Bake in slow oven 40 minutes. Remove from trays while still warm, cool on wire rack. Biscuit can be left plain or caramel can be drizzled over.

To make caramel: Combine ⅓ cup sugar and 2 tablespoons water in saucepan, stir over low heat until sugar is dissolved. Increase heat, boil until caramel in colour.

Makes approx. 4½ dozen.

Walnut Meringues

1 egg-white
¼ cup castor sugar
¼ cup brown sugar,
  firmly packed

½ cup chopped walnuts
1 teaspoon baking
  powder
2 oz. dark chocolate

Beat egg-white until soft peaks form, gradually add sugar, beat until dissolved. Fold in brown sugar, walnuts and sifted baking powder.

Drop dessertspoonfuls of mixture on to greased and lightly cornfloured tray. Bake in slow oven for approximately 1 hour. When cold, dip tops in melted chocolate.

Makes approx. 8.

Coffee Cream Meringues ✓

2 egg-whites
1½ cups castor sugar
½ teaspoon vanilla
1 teaspoon vinegar

1 teaspoon cornflour
4 tablespoons boiling
  water

Coffee Butter Cream:

2 teaspoons instant
  coffee powder
¼ pint hot water

8 oz. unsalted butter
1½ cups icing sugar

Combine all ingredients in small bowl of electric mixer, beat on high speed until mixture is very stiff (approximately 15 minutes). Spoon or pipe individual meringues, approximately 1½ in. in diameter, on to lightly greased trays which have been dusted with icing sugar.

Bake in moderate oven 20 minutes, reduce heat to slow and bake further 40 minutes. Allow to cool in oven. Sandwich meringues together with Coffee Butter Cream.

Coffee Butter Cream: Dissolve coffee in hot water; cool. Beat butter until soft and creamy, gradually beat in sifted icing sugar, beat until light and fluffy, add cold coffee; beat well.

Makes approx. 3 dozen meringues.

Almond and Date Meringues

3 oz. blanched almonds
6 oz. dates

2 egg-whites
1⅓ cups icing sugar

Beat egg-whites until soft peaks form. Gradually add sifted icing sugar, beat until very thick. Fold in finely chopped almonds and dates.

Drop teaspoonfuls on to aluminium foil-lined oven trays. Bake in very slow oven 30 minutes.

Makes approx. 3 dozen.

One-Egg Meringues

1 egg-white	1 teaspoon vanilla
1 cup castor sugar	2 teaspoons baking
2 tablespoons boiling	powder
water	1 teaspoon vinegar

Place egg-white and sugar in small bowl of electric mixer, beat 2 minutes on low speed. Add boiling water, vanilla and vinegar. Beat 15 minutes on medium speed to high speed. Fold in sifted baking powder.

Fill meringue mixture into piping bag; using star tube, pipe into small stars, on greased and cornfloured oven trays. Bake in very slow oven 1 hour. Decorate if desired, with little melted chocolate.

Makes approx. 3 dozen.

Easy Coconut Macaroons

1 cup coconut	1 egg
½ cup sugar	pinch salt
1 tablespoon cornflour	

Combine coconut, sugar and cornflour in bowl. Beat together egg and salt, stir into dry ingredients; mix well.

Place heaped teaspoonfuls of mixture on to greased and lightly cornfloured oven trays, press mixture lightly into peaked macaroon shape. Bake in moderate oven 15 minutes or until light golden brown. Remove from oven, loosen on trays immediately, allow to cool on trays.

Makes approx. 1½ dozen.

Coconut-Lemon Macaroons

2⅔ cups coconut	2 teaspoons grated
1 cup sugar	lemon rind
4 egg-whites	⅓ cup plain flour
1 tablespoon lemon juice	

In medium saucepan combine coconut, sugar, 1 egg-white, lemon rind and strained juice. Stir over low heat until lukewarm. Cool. Beat remaining egg-whites until soft peaks form. Gradually fold egg-whites into cooled mixture. Add sifted flour, combine gently.

Place mixture in heaped teaspoonfuls on to greased oven trays which have been lightly dusted with cornflour. Bake in slow oven 30 minutes, until firm and very lightly brown. Cool on trays.

Makes approx. 1½ dozen.

Almond Macaroons

4 oz. ground almonds	2 teaspoons plain flour
1 cup castor sugar	½ teaspoon vanilla
2 egg-whites	almond halves

Beat egg-whites until soft peaks form, gradually add sugar, beat until dissolved. Fold in ground almonds, sifted flour and vanilla.

Fill mixture into piping bag fitted with plain tube. Pipe small macaroons on to greased and cornfloured oven trays. Press almond half in centre of each macaroon. Bake in slow oven approximately 1 hour.

Makes approx. 1½ dozen.

Hazelnut Macaroons

Make as for Almond Macaroons, but substitute 4 oz. ground hazelnuts for the ground almonds, and sift ½ teaspoon instant coffee powder with the flour.

When cooked and cold, drizzle tops with a little melted chocolate; if desired, press a whole hazelnut into the chocolate before it sets.

Coconut Meringues

2 egg-whites	½ teaspoon vanilla
⅔ cup castor sugar	1 cup coconut
½ teaspoon cream of tartar	

Beat egg-whites until soft peaks form, add sugar gradually, beat until dissolved. Fold in sifted cream of tartar, vanilla and coconut.

Spoon or pipe mixture on to greased and lightly cornfloured oven tray. If desired, top with a small piece of red glacé cherry. Bake in very slow oven approximately 40 minutes or until dry to touch. Allow to cool in oven.

Makes approx. 1 dozen.

Favourite Biscuits

Amaretti

3 egg-whites	8 oz. marzipan meal
1 cup castor sugar	4 oz. dark chocolate

Beat egg-whites until soft peaks form; gradually add sugar, continue beating until sugar is dissolved. Fold in grated chocolate and sifted marzipan meal.

Drop teaspoonfuls on to greased and lightly cornfloured oven trays. Bake in moderately slow oven 12 to 15 minutes. Cool slightly on trays.

Makes approx. 4 dozen.

Coconut Oatmeal Cookies

1 cup shredded coconut	1 egg
4 oz. butter	1 teaspoon vanilla
1 cup brown sugar, lightly packed	1 cup rolled oats
	½ cup chopped nuts

Place coconut in shallow pan, stir constantly over medium heat until coconut is light golden brown; remove from pan immediately.

Cream butter, add sugar, beat until light and fluffy, add egg and vanilla; beat well. Stir in oats, nuts and coconut. Drop teaspoonfuls on to lightly greased and floured oven trays. Bake in moderate oven approximately 10 minutes; cool on trays.
Makes approximately 2 dozen.

Ground Rice Biscuits

4 oz. butter	½ cup ground rice
¾ cup castor sugar	1 cup plain flour
1 egg	

Beat butter until smooth, add sugar, beat until combined. Add beaten egg gradually, beat until light and creamy. Stir in sifted ground rice and flour.

Place mixture on to lightly floured surface, knead until smooth. Roll to ⅛ in. thickness, cut into rounds with 2 in. cutter. Place on lightly greased oven trays, bake in moderate oven 10 to 12 minutes. Cool on trays.

Makes approx. 3 dozen.

Honey Jumbles

4 oz. butter	1 cup plain flour
¾ cup brown sugar, lightly packed	3 teaspoons ground ginger
3 tablespoons honey	2 teaspoons mixed spice
1 egg	½ teaspoon ground cloves
1¼ cups self-raising flour	½ teaspoon bicarbonate of soda

Lemon Icing:

1½ cups icing sugar	1 tablespoon lemon juice, approx.
1 teaspoon butter	

Beat butter until soft, add sugar, beat until creamy, add honey and egg; beat well until combined. Stir in sifted dry ingredients.

Place mixture into forcing bag, fitted with plain tube, ½ in. in diameter. Pipe mixture into 2½ in. lengths on to lightly greased oven trays, allow room for spreading. Bake in moderate oven 12 to 15 minutes, cool on trays. When cold, top with lemon icing.

Lemon Icing: Sift icing sugar into small heat-proof basin, add softened butter and enough lemon juice to give a stiff paste. Stir constantly over hot water to spreading consistency.

Makes approx. 2½ dozen.

Peanut Roughs

¾ cup self-raising flour	4 oz. salted peanuts
2 cups rolled oats	4 oz. butter
1 cup brown sugar, lightly packed	2 tablespoons golden syrup
	1 egg

Sift flour into basin, add oats, brown sugar and roughly chopped peanuts; mix well. Melt butter, add golden syrup and beaten egg; add to dry ingredients; mix well.

Drop teaspoonfuls of mixture on to lightly greased oven trays, bake in moderate oven 12 to 15 minutes, or until golden brown.

Makes approx. 4 dozen.

From left to right, in front of barrow: at top, Coconut-Lemon Macaroon, Coconut Meringue, Easy Coconut Macaroon; below, Hazelnut Macaroon, Almond Macaroon.

Raspberry Nougat Cookies

1½ cups self-raising flour	1 egg-yolk
3 oz. butter	2 tablespoons water, approx.
2 tablespoons sugar	

Topping:

1 egg-white	½ cup sugar
1 cup coconut	2 tablespoons milk
2 oz. ground almonds	raspberry jam

Sift flour into basin, rub in butter; add sugar. Add egg-yolk and enough water to give a soft dough. Knead on floured surface until smooth, roll to ⅛ in. thickness, cut into 2 in. rounds with cutter. Place on lightly greased oven trays.

Place level teaspoonfuls of coconut mixture on to each round of dough, make small indentation in top, spoon in small amount of jam. Bake in moderate oven 12 to 15 minutes, or until lightly browned.

Topping: Beat egg-white until soft peaks form, fold in dry ingredients and milk.

Makes approx. 3 dozen.

Almond Meringue Shortbread

¾ cup plain flour	¼ cup castor sugar
½ cup self-raising flour	2 tablespoons castor sugar, extra
2 oz. marzipan meal	
4 oz. butter	1 oz. blanched almonds
1 egg, separated	3 tablespoons apricot jam

Sift flours and marzipan meal. Rub in butter until mixture resembles fine breadcrumbs. Add sugar and egg-yolk, mix well, knead until smooth. Press mixture into base of well-greased, 7 in. x 11 in. lamington tin. Spread over warmed, sieved apricot jam.

Beat egg-white until soft peaks form, beat in extra castor sugar, beat until firm peaks form. Spread meringue over jam, sprinkle chopped almonds on top. Bake in moderately slow oven 35 to 40 minutes. Cut into slices while warm.

Cool in tin before turning out.

Passionfruit Slice

4 oz. butter	¼ cup cornflour
½ cup icing sugar	1 egg
¾ cup self-raising flour	3 passionfruit
1 cup plain flour	

Passionfruit Icing:

1 cup icing sugar	1 oz. butter
2 passionfruit	

Cream butter and sugar until light and fluffy. Add egg, beat well. Mix in sifted dry ingredients alternately with passionfruit pulp. Press mixture into well-greased 7 in. x 11 in. lamington tin.

Bake in moderately slow oven 30 minutes, until lightly brown. Cool in tin before turning out. When cold, spread Passionfruit Icing thinly on top. Cut into squares or slices.

Passionfruit Icing: Melt butter over low heat. Remove from heat, add sifted icing sugar and passionfruit pulp. Beat well until smooth.

Sultana Coconut Cookies

1 cup plain flour	¾ cup cornflakes
1 teaspoon mixed spice	¾ cup sultanas
¼ teaspoon bicarbonate of soda	4 oz. butter
	1 egg
¾ cup coconut	1 tablespoon golden syrup
¾ cup sugar	

Sift flour, spice and soda into basin, add remaining dry ingredients; mix well. Add melted butter to well in centre of dry ingredients, then combined beaten egg and golden syrup; mix well. Drop teaspoonfuls of mixture on to lightly greased oven trays, bake in moderate oven 10 to 15 minutes, or until golden brown; cool on trays.

Makes approx. 3 dozen.

Chocolate Cream Cookies

4 oz. butter	2 tablespoons cocoa
1 teaspoon vanilla	strawberry jam
⅓ cup sugar	whipped cream
1 egg	icing sugar
2 cups self-raising flour	

Beat butter and vanilla until creamy; add sugar, beat until just combined. Add egg, beat well. Stir in sifted dry ingredients. Turn on to floured surface, knead lightly until smooth, roll to ⅛ in. thickness, cut into rounds with 2 in. cutter.

Place on lightly greased oven trays, bake in moderate oven 10 to 12 minutes, cool on trays. When cold, join together with jam and cream, dust tops with icing sugar.

Makes approx. 2 dozen complete biscuits.

Sesame Biscuits

¾ cup self-raising flour	1 egg-yolk
1¼ cups plain flour	1 teaspoon vanilla
¼ teaspoon salt	1 tablespoon milk
6 oz. butter	4 oz. toasted sesame
¾ cup castor sugar	seeds

Sift flours and salt into bowl. Rub in butter until mixture resembles fine breadcrumbs; add sugar, egg-yolk, vanilla and milk, mix to a soft dough.

Take teaspoonfuls of mixture, roll into balls the size of a walnut. Roll in sesame seeds, put on greased oven trays, press down with back of spoon. Bake in moderate oven 12 to 15 minutes.

Makes approx. 4 dozen.

To Toast Sesame Seeds: Put in a small pan, stir constantly over heat 5 minutes.

Sour Cream Cookies

2 oz. butter	1 egg
2 teaspoons grated	½ teaspoon bicarbonate
lemon rind	of soda
1 cup castor sugar	pinch salt
½ cup sour cream	raisins
1⅓ cups plain flour	extra castor sugar

Cream butter and lemon rind, add sugar, beat well; add egg, beat until light and fluffy. Stir in sour cream alternately with combined sifted flour, soda and salt.

Drop teaspoonfuls of mixture on to greased oven trays, about 2 in. apart, to allow room for spreading. Place a whole raisin in centre of each biscuit, sprinkle lightly with extra castor sugar. Bake in moderate oven 10 to 15 minutes.

Makes approx. 2½ dozen.

Burnt Butter Biscuits

4 oz. butter	1 egg
⅔ cup sugar	1 teaspoon vanilla
1½ cups self-raising flour	1 oz. blanched almonds

Melt butter in saucepan, cook gently until brown in colour. Cool. Add sugar, beat well. Stir in egg and vanilla, beat well. Add sifted flour, mix to stiff consistency.

Roll into small balls, about 1 in. in diameter; place on greased trays, top with half an almond. Bake in a moderate oven 10 to 12 minutes until golden brown. Cool on trays.

Makes approx. 4 dozen.

Continental Almond Rounds

1½ cups plain flour	1 tablespoon sugar
½ cup self-raising flour	1 egg-yolk
4 oz. butter	¼ cup milk, approx.

Icing:

1 egg-white	2 oz. slivered almonds
¾ cup icing sugar	

Sift dry ingredients into bowl; rub in butter. Stir in egg-yolk and enough milk to make a stiff paste. Roll out thinly on lightly floured surface, to about ⅛ in. thickness; spread with icing, cut into small rounds or 1 in. x 3 in. fingers.

Transfer to ungreased oven trays. Bake in moderate oven 12 minutes or until lightly brown. Leave on tray a few minutes, cool on wire rack.

Icing: Beat egg-white slightly, add sifted icing sugar, beat until smooth. Stir in almonds.

Makes approx. 3½ dozen.

Currant Fingers

Pastry:

2½ cups plain flour	½ cup iced water, approx.
pinch salt	1 egg-white for glazing
6 oz. butter	castor sugar

Filling:

3 oz. butter	1 tablespoon marmalade
⅓ cup brown sugar,	1 tablespoon plain flour
firmly packed	1 teaspoon cinnamon
1 tablespoon golden syrup	12 oz. currants

Pastry: Sift flour and salt into basin, grate butter over flour, stir in with a knife, stir in enough water with knife to give a firm, pliable dough. Refrigerate 30 minutes.

Roll out two-thirds of pastry to line base and sides of greased 7 in. x 11 in. lamington tin, spread evenly with cold filling, top with remaining pastry. Glaze top lightly with beaten egg-white, sprinkle with castor sugar.

Bake in moderately hot oven 25 minutes or until golden-brown. When cold, remove from tin and cut into fingers.

Filling: Combine all ingredients in saucepan, stir over low heat until butter is melted and ingredients combined. Allow mixture to become cold.

Shortbread

Shortbread

2 cups plain flour	1 tablespoon ground rice
¼ cup icing sugar	6 oz. butter

Sift flour, sugar and ground rice into bowl. Rub in butter, knead until mixture is smooth. Press mixture into two ungreased 7 in. round sandwich tins. Pinch edges, cut each round into 8 triangles with sharp knife. Prick with fork.

Bake in moderately slow oven 30 minutes, until very lightly brown. Cool in tins before turning out.

Shortbread may also be shaped in mould. Press prepared mixture firmly into mould, invert on to ungreased baking tray. Remove mould and bake as above.

Ayrshire Shortbread

1 cup plain flour	1 egg-yolk
⅔ cup ground rice	2 tablespoons cream
4 oz. butter	extra castor sugar
½ cup castor sugar	

Sift flour and ground rice into bowl, rub in butter. Add sugar, mix well. Mix to a stiff dough with egg-yolk and cream. Knead lightly on floured surface, roll out to ¼ in. thickness. Cut into rounds with 2 in. cutter; prick well with fork.

Place on lightly greased oven trays, bake in moderate oven approximately 15 minutes or until pale golden. Sprinkle with extra castor sugar. Cool on trays.

Makes approx. 2½ dozen.

Almond Fingers

8 oz. butter	2½ cups plain flour
½ cup castor sugar	1 egg-white
2 teaspoons grated lemon rind	2 oz. slivered almonds
	2 tablespoons sugar, extra

Cream butter, castor sugar and lemon rind, until light and fluffy; fold in sifted flour. Beat egg-white until soft peaks form, gradually fold into creamed mixture.

Place into greased 7 in. x 11 in. lamington tin, spread evenly with spatula. Sprinkle with sugar and almonds. Bake in moderate oven ¾ hour. Cut while hot; cool in tin.

Scotch Shortbread

7 oz. butter	2¼ cups plain flour
½ teaspoon vanilla	¼ cup ground rice
⅓ cup castor sugar	

Cream butter and vanilla until light and fluffy, gradually beat in sugar. Work in sifted dry ingredients. Knead well on lightly floured surface until smooth.

Press into lightly greased 7 in. x 11 in. lamington tin, cut into bars and prick each bar decoratively with fork. Bake in slow oven 50 to 60 minutes.

Or divide mixture into two, roll each portion out to form 7 in. circle, pinch edges decoratively. Mark into wedges. Place on greased oven trays, bake in slow oven approximately 45 minutes.

Chocolate Fudge Shortbread

Base:

4 oz. butter	1½ cups plain flour
¼ cup castor sugar	

Fudge:

4 oz. butter	2 tablespoons golden syrup
½ cup castor sugar	⅔ cup condensed milk

Chocolate Icing:

2 oz. dark chocolate	1 oz. butter

Base: Cream butter and sugar together until light and fluffy. Sift flour, gradually add to creamed mixture, making into firm dough. Press into greased 7 in. square slab tin.

Bake in moderate oven 20 to 25 minutes, until golden brown. Cool in tin.

Fudge: Place all ingredients into saucepan, bring slowly to the boil, stirring constantly. Simmer gently 4 minutes without stirring (mixture will catch a little on base of saucepan). Pour over shortbread, allow to cool.

Chocolate Icing: Melt chocolate in basin over saucepan of hot water, add butter, stir well. Spread chocolate icing over cool fudge; when set, cut into squares.

Scotch Shortbread can be baked in a round and cut into wedges, or baked in a special mould; see page 22.

Savoury Biscuits

Cheese Straws

1¼ cups plain flour
2 oz. butter
3 oz. cheese
pinch cayenne pepper
¼ teaspoon salt
1 egg-yolk
1 tablespoon lemon juice

Rub butter into sifted flour until mixture resembles fine breadcrumbs. Add grated cheese, cayenne and salt; mix lightly. Combine egg-yolk and lemon juice; make a well in centre of dry ingredients, add egg-yolk mixture; mix to a firm dough.

Roll pastry to ¼ in. thickness, cut into strips 3 in. x ¼in. Place on to greased oven trays, bake in moderate oven approximately 12 minutes, or until pale golden brown.

Makes approx. 10 dozen.

Cheese Blisters ✓

1 cup self-raising flour
½ teaspoon salt
pinch cayenne pepper
½ oz butter
2 oz. cheese
2 tablespoons mayonnaise
extra salt

Sift together flour, salt and cayenne, rub in butter. Add grated cheese, mix to a firm dough with mayonnaise. Roll dough out to ⅛ in. thickness, cut out with round cutter.

Place on lightly greased oven trays, sprinkle lightly with salt. Bake in moderate oven 10 to 12 minutes. Cool on trays.

Makes approx. 3 dozen.

Cheese and Potato Biscuits

¾ cup plain flour
2 oz. butter
½ cup cooked mashed potato
½ teaspoon salt
4 oz. cheese
1 egg

Sift flour into bowl; rub in butter. Stir in salt, mashed potato, and 2 oz. of the grated cheese; blend well. Roll out to ⅛ in. thickness on lightly floured board.

Cut into rounds, using 2 in. cutter. Place rounds on greased oven trays, brush each with beaten egg and sprinkle with remaining grated cheese. Bake in moderate oven approximately 12 to 15 minutes or until light golden brown. When cold, store in airtight tin.

Makes approx. 3 dozen.

Cream Cheese Biscuits

1 cup self-raising flour
½ teaspoon salt
pinch pepper
1 oz. butter
2 oz. packaged cream cheese
2 tablespoons cold water, approx.

Sift dry ingredients into bowl, rub in butter and cheese; mix to a dry dough with water. Roll out to ⅛ in. thickness on lightly floured board. Cut into rounds, using 2½ in. cutter.

Place on greased oven trays; prick with fork. Bake in hot oven 8 to 10 minutes until crisp and lightly browned.

Makes approx. 3 dozen.

Walnut and Cheese Biscuits

3 oz. butter
3 oz. cheese
¾ cup plain flour
salt, pepper
1 egg
4 oz. walnuts
pinch nutmeg

Rub butter into sifted flour, add grated cheese and seasonings; mix well. Take teaspoonfuls of mixture and roll into balls. Roll in beaten egg, then in finely chopped walnuts.

Bake on lightly greased oven trays in moderately hot oven 15 minutes.

Makes approx. 2 dozen.

Flaky Cheese Biscuits

2 oz. butter
2 oz. cheese
½ egg-yolk
salt
¼ teaspoon paprika
½ cup plain flour

Beat butter until creamy, gradually add finely grated cheese, egg-yolk, salt and paprika. Work in sifted flour. When well blended, refrigerate 1 hour.

Knead lightly, roll out on floured board to ¼ in. thickness. Cut out in 1 in. rounds; place on lightly greased oven trays, bake in hot oven 10 minutes.

Make approx. 2½ dozen.

Paprika Biscuits

3 oz. butter	½ teaspoon salt
3 oz. cheese	½ teaspoon dry mustrad
1 cup plain flour	2 teaspoons poppy
1 teaspoon paprika	seeds

Beat together butter and grated cheese until soft and creamy. Sift together dry ingredients, add to cheese mixture, beat until well blended.

Take dessertspoonfuls of mixture and roll into small balls, using floured hands. Place on greased oven tray, flatten slightly, sprinkle poppy seeds lightly over each biscuit. Bake in moderate oven 15 to 20 minutes or until lightly golden brown. Loosen and cool on tray.

Makes approx. 1½ dozen.

Cheese and Sesame Wafers

1 cup plain flour	2 oz. cheese
½ teaspoon salt	⅓ cup toasted
pinch pepper	sesame seeds
½ teaspoon dry mustard	1 egg-yolk
½ teaspoon ground ginger	2 oz. butter
½ teaspoon sugar	1 tablespoon water

Sift dry ingredients into bowl. Stir in grated cheese and toasted sesame seeds. Combine lightly beaten egg-yolk, melted butter and water. Stir into dry ingredients; form into a ball. Wrap in greaseproof paper; refrigerate 30 minutes.

Roll out to ⅛ in. thickness on lightly floured board. Cut into 1 in. x 2 in. strips or 2 in. squares. Place on ungreased oven trays, bake in moderate oven 15 minutes. Cool on trays.

Makes approx. 4½ dozen.

To toast sesame seeds: Place seeds in small saucepan, stir over heat for 5 to 7 minutes.

Coconut Cheese Balls

2 oz. cheese	salt, pepper
1 cup plain flour	coconut
3 oz. butter	

Grate cheese, combine with sifted flour, salt and pepper. Rub in butter, work mixture until smooth. Roll into small balls, roll in coconut. Place on greased oven trays. Bake in moderately slow oven 15 minutes.

Makes approx. 1½ dozen.

Cheese Biscuits ✓

1 cup plain flour	4 oz. grated parmesan
4 oz. butter	cheese

Sift flour into basin, add cheese, rub in butter until fine. Press ingredients together lightly. Place on lightly floured surface, work with hands until smooth. Roll to ⅛ in. thickness on lightly floured board, cut into rounds with 2 in. cutter. Place on lightly greased oven trays, bake in moderate oven 10 minutes, or until light golden brown; cool on trays.

Makes approx. 3 dozen.

Curry Biscuits

1 cup plain flour	pinch cayenne pepper
¼ teaspoon salt	3 oz. butter
½ teaspoon dry mustard	3 oz. grated cheese
1½ teaspoons curry	1 egg-yolk
powder	1 tablespoon milk

Sift dry ingredients into basin, rub in butter, add cheese, mix well. Add beaten egg-yolk and milk, mix to firm dough. Roll to ⅛ in. thickness on lightly floured surface, cut into rounds with 2 in. cutter. Place on greased oven trays, bake in moderately hot oven 10 minutes, or until lightly browned; cool on trays.

Makes approx. 2 dozen.

Cheese Puffs ✓

1 cup plain flour	2 oz. finely grated
1 teaspoon salt	cheese
pinch pepper	¼ cup water approx.
2 oz. butter	

Sift flour and seasonings into basin, rub in butter; add cheese. Stir in enough water to make a soft pliable dough. Place on lightly floured surface, knead until smooth; divide dough in half.

Roll half the dough to 14 in. square. Fold up the bottom third of dough, fold the top third down over it. Then fold crossways in half, roll again to 14 in. square; repeat folding. Roll again to 14 in. square; dough should be almost paper thin.

Cut into rounds with 2 in. cutter, place on lightly greased oven trays, bake in hot oven 5 to 8 minutes, or until golden brown and puffy.

Repeat with remaining dough.

Note: These are unusual, quite delicious little biscuits; they puff up in the baking, like puff pastry. Makes approx. 5 dozen.

Old Fashioned Favourites

Melting Moments

4 oz. butter	½ cup cornflour
2 tablespoons icing sugar	½ cup plain flour

Orange Cream:

1 oz. butter	2 teaspoons orange
3 tablespoons icing sugar	juice
1 teaspoon grated orange rind	

Cream butter and sifted icing sugar until light and fluffy. Add sifted flours, mix well.

Put mixture into piping bag with fluted tube. Pipe small stars on to lightly greased trays, bake in moderate oven 10 to 12 minutes or until pale golden brown. Cool on trays. Join with Orange Cream.

Orange Cream: Beat butter until smooth, gradually add sifted icing sugar, beat until mixture is light and creamy. Beat in orange rind and juice.

Makes approx. 1 dozen complete biscuits.

Monte Carlos

4 oz. butter	1 teaspoon vanilla
½ cup sugar	2 cups self-raising flour
1 egg	¾ cup plain flour

Filling:

2 oz. butter	2 teaspoons milk
¾ cup icing sugar	raspberry jam
½ teaspoon vanilla	

Cream butter and sugar until light and fluffy; add egg and vanilla, beat well. Add sifted dry ingredients; mix well. Put teaspoonfuls of mixture on to greased oven trays, press each biscuit down lightly with back of fork. Bake in moderate oven 10 to 12 minutes or until golden brown. When cold, join with raspberry jam and filling.

Filling: Cream butter and sifted icing sugar until light and fluffy, add vanilla, gradually add milk; beat well.

Makes approx. 3½ to 4 dozen complete biscuits.

Jam Drops

4 oz. butter	½ cup plain flour
¼ cup sugar	¼ cup arrowroot
1 egg	pinch salt
2 teaspoons honey	raspberry jam
1 cup self-raising flour	

Cream butter and sugar until light and fluffy; add egg and honey, beat well. Sift dry ingredients, add to creamed mixture, mix well.

Roll teaspoonfuls of mixture into balls, put on greased oven trays. With finger, make small indentation in centre of each biscuit; put approximately ¼ teaspoon of raspberry jam into each indentation. Bake in moderate oven 12 to 15 minutes or until a light golden brown.

Makes approx. 3 dozen.

Chinese Chews

½ cup self-raising flour	2 teaspoons grated
½ cup plain flour	lemon rind
1 teaspoon mixed spice	1 egg
1 cup sugar	2 tablespoons milk
2 oz. chopped walnuts	1 oz. butter
or mixed nuts	½ teaspoon vanilla
4 oz. chopped dates	

Sift together flours, mixed spice and sugar. Mix in nuts, dates and lemon rind. Add beaten egg, milk, melted butter and vanilla; mix well.

Spread in greased 7 in. x 11 in. lamington tin. Bake in moderate oven 30 to 35 minutes. Cut into fingers while hot.

Yo-Yo Biscuits

3 oz. butter	¾ cup plain flour
2 tablespoons icing sugar	2½ tablespoons custard powder

Cream butter and sifted icing sugar until light and fluffy. Add sifted flour and custard powder; mix well. Roll teaspoonfuls of mixture into small balls, put on greased oven trays, press each down lightly with back of fork. Bake in moderate oven 10 to 15 minutes.

Makes approx. 2 dozen.

Florentines, see page 34.

Health Biscuits

Crunchy Wholemeal Biscuits

2½ cups wholemeal
  self-raising flour
¾ cup coconut
1 cup raw sugar
6 oz. butter

¾ cup chopped
  mixed fruit
1 teaspoon vanilla
2 eggs

Sift flour into mixing bowl, rub in butter; stir in coconut, sugar and mixed fruit. Beat eggs and vanilla together lightly, stir into dry mixture, mix to a firm dough. Turn out on to floured board, knead lightly.

Roll out to ¼ in. thickness, cut into rounds, using 1½ in. floured cutter. Place on greased oven trays approximately 2 in. apart, bake in moderate oven 10 to 12 minutes or until golden brown. Loosen; cool on trays.

Makes approx. 5 dozen.

Wholemeal Date Slice

Pastry:

1½ cups wholemeal
  plain flour
1¼ cups wholemeal
  self-raising flour
pinch salt
5 oz. butter

1 tablespoon honey
1 egg
⅓ cup milk
sugar
extra milk

Filling:

1 lb. dates
½ cup water
2 teaspoons grated
  lemon rind

2 tablespoons lemon
  juice

Pastry: Sift flours and salt into bowl, rub in butter until mixture resembles fine breadcrumbs. Combine honey, egg and milk, add to dry ingredients, mix to a firm dough. Knead lightly on floured surface.

Divide dough in halves, roll one portion to fit base of greased 7 in. x 11 in. lamington tin. Spread with cold date mixture, cover with remaining rolled-out pastry. Glaze with a little milk or water, sprinkle with sugar.

Bake in moderately hot oven 25 to 30 minutes. Allow to cool in tin, cut into squares.

Filling: Chop dates, place in saucepan with water, lemon rind and juice; cook, stirring, until mixture is thick and smooth; cool.

Date and Walnut Slice

1 cup wholemeal
  self-raising flour
4 oz. chopped dates
½ cup raw sugar

2 oz. chopped walnuts
1 egg
2 oz. butter

Combine sifted flour, dates, sugar and walnuts. Make well in centre, add beaten egg and melted butter; mix well.

Spoon mixture into greased 8 in. square slab tin. Bake in moderate oven 30 to 35 minutes. Cut into slices or squares while still hot; cool in tin.

Raisin Crunchies

3 oz. butter
½ cup raw sugar
1 egg
1 cup chopped raisins

2½ cups wholemeal
  self-raising flour
¼ cup milk

Cream butter and sugar until light, add egg; beat well. Add fruit, then add sifted flour and milk alternately; mix well.

Roll teaspoonfuls of mixture into balls, put on greased oven trays , and flatten lightly with a fork. Bake in moderate oven 12 to 15 minutes; loosen with a knife, cool on trays.

Makes 1½ dozen.

Crispies

4 oz. butter
2 teaspoons treacle
2 tablespoons water
1 cup wholemeal
  self-raising flour

1 cup coconut
1 cup rolled oats
1 cup raw sugar

Melt butter over low heat, add treacle, and water. Sift flour, add remaining ingredients, make well in centre, pour in butter-liquid; mix well.

Form teaspoonfuls of mixture into balls, put on greased oven trays, flatten slightly with a fork. Bake in moderate oven 12 to 15 minutes; loosen with a knife, cool on trays.

Makes approx. 1½ dozen.

Sesame Seed Fingers

2 eggs
¾ cup raw sugar
½ cup chopped raisins
½ cup sultanas
½ cup chopped dried apricots
1 cup sesame meal
½ cup chopped dates
⅓ cup wholemeal plain flour
2 tablespoons wheatgerm

Beat eggs and sugar until light in colour and thick. Fold in all remaining ingredients, mix well. Spread mixture into greased 7 in. x 11 in. lamington tin.

Bake in moderate oven 20 to 25 minutes. Cut into fingers while hot, allow to cool in tin.

Apple Oatmeal Cookies

4 oz. butter
1 cup raw sugar
2 eggs
¾ cup rolled oats
1¼ cups wholemeal self-raising flour
4 oz. walnuts
1 medium apple

Cream butter and sugar until light and fluffy, add eggs one at a time, beating well after each addition. Fold in sifted flour and rolled oats. Add chopped walnuts, and peeled and grated apple; mix well.

Drop teaspoonfuls of mixture on to greased oven trays, allow room for spreading. Bake in moderate oven 12 to 15 minutes or until golden-brown.

Makes approx. 3½ dozen.

Honey Peanut Biscuits

4 oz. butter
¾ cup raw sugar
1 egg
½ cup peanut butter
2 teaspoons honey
¼ cup wheatgerm
½ cup wholemeal self-raising flour
¾ cup wholemeal plain flour
extra raw sugar

Cream butter and sugar until light and fluffy, add egg; beat well. Add peanut butter and honey; beat well. Fold in sifted flours, and wheatgerm.

Take teaspoonfuls of mixture, roll into balls, place on greased oven trays, flatten each ball with the bottom of a glass dipped in raw sugar. Bake in moderate oven 8 to 10 minutes or until golden-brown.

Makes approx. 3½ dozen.

Apricot Bar Cookies

⅔ cup honey
⅓ cup oil
6 oz. dried apricots
1 cup sultanas
½ cup sunflower seeds
¼ cup orange juice
1 cup wholemeal self-raising flour
¾ cup rolled oats
½ cup wheatgerm

Combine honey, oil, chopped apricots, sultanas, sunflower seeds, and orange juice in a bowl. Add sifted flour, rolled oats and wheatgerm, mix well.

Spread into greased 9 in. square slab tin. Bake in moderate oven 25 to 30 minutes, or until light golden-brown. Cut into squares while still warm. Allow to cool in tin.

Fruit Bars

1 egg
2 tablespoons raw sugar
1 cup chopped mixed fruit
½ cup chopped dates
2 tablespoons honey
2 oz. butter
½ cup wheatgerm
½ cup coconut
1 cup cornflakes
1 cup wholemeal plain flour

Beat egg and sugar together, add fruit; mix well. Melt butter, add honey, add to fruit mixture with sifted flour and remaining dry ingredients.

Press into greased 7 in. x 11 in. lamington tin. Bake in moderate oven 15 minutes. Cut into bars when still warm.

Sugar 'n' Spice Cookies

4 oz. butter
½ teaspoon vanilla
¾ cup raw sugar
1 egg
¼ cup wheatgerm
1 cup wholemeal plain flour
¼ cup wholemeal self-raising flour
½ cup raw sugar, extra
1 teaspoon cinnamon

Beat butter and vanilla until creamy, add sugar; beat well. Add egg, beat only until combined, stir in wheatgerm. Stir in sifted flours. Roll mixture into balls, ¾ in. in diameter, toss in combined extra sugar and cinnamon. Place on greased oven trays, bake in moderate oven 10 minutes; cool on wire rack.

Makes approx. 3 dozen.

International Biscuits

French Butter Biscuits

4 oz. butter	1 egg-yolk
½ cup icing sugar	½ teaspoon vanilla
1 cup plain flour	apricot or strawberry jam
½ cup self-raising flour	

Cream together butter and sifted icing sugar until light and fluffy; add vanilla. Sift flours together, beat into creamed mixture with lightly beaten egg-yolk, mix well to form soft dough. Refrigerate dough several hours or overnight.

Roll out on well-floured board to approximately ¼ in. thick. Cut into rounds, using 2 in. floured fluted cutter. Cut another small round in the centres of half the biscuits. Place on ungreased oven trays, bake in moderate oven 10 to 15 minutes. Remove from oven, allow to cool on trays.

Sieve a little warmed apricot or strawberry jam, spread a little on bottom half of biscuits (the ones without centre cut-outs).

Sandwich together with top round. Dust over a little sifted icing sugar before serving.

Makes approx. 2 dozen complete biscuits.

Linzer Biscuits

⅔ cup plain flour	1 egg, separated
⅔ cup castor sugar	1 egg-yolk, hard-boiled
6 oz. finely	1 oz. chopped walnuts
chopped walnuts	extra
¼ teaspoon grated	icing sugar
lemon rind	raspberry jam
3 oz. butter	

Place sifted flour, sugar, walnuts, lemon rind and hard-boiled egg-yolk in bowl. Rub in butter, add uncooked egg-yolk. Knead lightly on floured board, roll out to ¼ in. thickness.

Cut into 3 in. rounds with fluted cutter. From half these rounds cut out a small fluted circle from centre. Place on greased baking trays, brush tops of holed biscuits with lightly beaten egg-white, sprinkle with extra chopped walnuts. Bake in moderately slow oven 15 minutes. When cool, sandwich together with raspberry jam (one plain biscuit topped with one holed biscuit); sprinkle with sifted icing sugar.

Makes 14 complete biscuits.

Swiss Cakes

8 oz. butter	2 cups plain flour
½ teaspoon vanilla	raspberry jam or
2 tablespoons castor	glacé cherries
sugar	icing sugar

Beat butter until white and creamy, add vanilla and sugar, beat until light and fluffy. Stir in half the sifted flour, then remaining half; do not beat. Place mixture into piping bag fitted with large fluted tube. Place paper patty cases into patty pans, then pipe mixture into cases. Bake in moderate oven 20 minutes.

When cold, remove from tins, place a small dot of jam or a piece of glacé cherry on each biscuit, then dust lightly with sifted icing sugar.

Makes approx. 1½ dozen.

Viennese Biscuits

8 oz. butter	2 cups plain flour
¼ cup castor sugar	pinch salt
½ teaspoon vanilla	

Cream together butter and sugar until light and fluffy. Add vanilla and carefully fold in sifted flour and salt. Fill into piping bag fitted with fluted tube. Pipe into finger lengths on lightly greased oven trays.

Bake in moderate oven 15 to 20 minutes. Cool on trays. Leave plain, or dip one end in melted chocolate for pretty effect.

Makes approx. 3 dozen.

At back, Linzer Biscuits and Viennese Biscuits; in front, Swiss Cakes.

No-Bake Biscuits

White Christmas

8 oz. solid white
   vegetable shortening
3 cups rice bubbles
1 cup coconut
¾ cup icing sugar
1 cup full-cream
   milk powder

1 oz mixed peel
1 oz. preserved ginger
1 oz. glacé apricots
1 oz. glacé pineapple
¼ cup sultanas
1 oz. glacé cherries

Melt chopped white vegetable shortening over gentle heat. Combine rice bubbles, coconut, sifted icing sugar, powdered milk and chopped fruits; mix well. Add melted shortening and mix thoroughly.

Press mixture into lightly greased and paper-lined 7 in. x 11 in. lamington tin. Refrigerate until firm, cut into bars for serving.

Chocolate Fruit Squares

½ cup drinking chocolate
1½ cups coconut
1 cup sultanas
1 cup crushed cornflakes
1 oz. chopped walnuts

½ cup finely crushed
   plain sweet biscuits
¾ cup condensed milk
1 tablespoon sherry
4 oz. dark chocolate

Combine drinking chocolate, coconut, sultanas, cornflakes, walnuts and crushed biscuits. Add condensed milk and sherry, mix well to a stiff spreading consistency. Spread mixture over base of lightly greased and paper-lined 7 in. x 11 in. lamington tin. Refrigerate 1 hour, turn out of tin, remove paper.

Roughly chop chocolate, melt over hot water. Spread melted chocolate over fruit base, mark decoratively with fork. Allow chocolate to set, cut into squares for serving.

Chocolate Date Fingers

4 oz. butter
½ cup sugar
4 oz. chopped dates
3 cups rice bubbles

3 oz. dark chocolate
½ oz. solid white
   vegetable shortening

Melt butter in saucepan, add sugar and dates. Stir over heat until mixture boils and thickens. Remove from heat, stir in rice bubbles, mix thoroughly. Press mixture firmly into 7 in. x 11 in. lamington tin which has been lined with aluminium foil. Refrigerate until firm, turn out of tin, remove foil.

Melt chopped chocolate and white vegetable shortening over hot water (do not overheat); spread over base, mark decoratively with fork. Cut into fingers when chocolate is firm.

Chocolate Biscuit Slice

1 lb. icing sugar
2 tablespoons cocoa
6 oz. solid white
   vegetable shortening

1 teaspoon vanilla
1 egg
½ lb. plain biscuits
   in oblong shape

Remove biscuits from their wrapping, let stand overnight, exposed to the air, so that they soften slightly.

Combine in bowl sifted icing sugar and cocoa, egg, vanilla. Melt shortening over gentle heat, pour into bowl. Mix thoroughly till smooth and just beginning to thicken.

Arrange alternate layers of chocolate mixture and biscuits in greased and lined 6 in. square cake tin, commencing and finishing with a chocolate layer. Cover, refrigerate until set. Remove from tin, cut into slices.

Cornflake Chews

¾ cup brown sugar,
   firmly packed
⅓ cup golden syrup

½ oz. butter
2 cups cornflakes
4 oz. salted peanuts

Combine sugar, golden syrup and butter in saucepan, stir constantly over medium heat until sugar dissolves. Bring to boil, immediately remove from heat. Stir in cornflakes and peanuts.

Drop teaspoonfuls of mixture into paper patty cases. Refrigerate until firm.

Makes approx. 2½ dozen.

Chocolate Crackles

4 cups rice bubbles
1 cup coconut
⅔ cup cocoa

1½ cups icing sugar
8 oz. solid white
   vegetable shortening

Stir chopped vegetable shortening over low heat until melted; it is important that the shortening is not over-heated. Combine rice bubbles, coconut, sifted cocoa and sifted icing sugar in a bowl. Add melted vegetable shortening, mix well. Spoon mixture into paper patty cases. Refrigerate until set.

Makes approx. 3 dozen.

Continental Chocolate Slice

4 oz. butter	1 teaspoon vanilla
½ cup sugar	½ lb. wheatmeal biscuits
1½ tablespoons cocoa	¾ cup coconut
1 egg	2 oz. chopped walnuts

Topping:

2 oz. butter	2 tablespoons hot water
2 cups icing sugar	4 oz. dark chocolate
1 tablespoon custard powder	

Crush biscuits into fine crumbs. Combine butter, sugar and cocoa in saucepan. Stir over low heat until well blended. Stir in beaten egg and vanilla.

Cook, stirring, 1 minute. Remove from heat, stir in biscuit crumbs, coconut, and walnuts, mix well. Press mixture into greased 7 in. x 11 in. lamington tin, refrigerate until set.

Topping: Cream butter well. Sift together icing sugar and custard powder, add to butter alternately with hot water. Beat until light and fluffy. Spread over biscuit base, refrigerate.

Melt chopped chocolate over hot water, spread evenly over firm, cold topping; refrigerate.

Choc-Mint Slices

Base:

1 cup lightly crushed cornflakes	⅓ cup brown sugar, lightly packed
½ cup coconut	4 oz. butter

Peppermint Layer:

1½ cups icing sugar	2 tablespoons milk
1 oz. solid white vegetable shortening	¼ teaspoon peppermint essence

Base: Combine dry ingredients in basin, add melted butter; mix well. Spread evenly over base of greased 7 in. x 11 in. lamington tin, refrigerate 30 minutes. Top evenly with Peppermint Layer, refrigerate until set, top with Chocolate Icing. Refrigerate until firm, cut into small squares.

Peppermint Layer: Melt shortening over low heat, add to sifted icing sugar, add milk; mix well, add peppermint essence.

Chocolate Icing: Melt 3 oz. solid white vegetable shortening over very low heat, blend in ½ cup sifted drinking chocolate, stir well; cool slightly before spreading.

Lemon Date Bars

8 oz. dates	1 teaspoon vanilla
½ cup sugar	½ cup coconut
2 oz. butter	3 cups rice bubbles
1 tablespoon lemon juice	2 oz. chopped peanuts

Chop dates, combine in saucepan with butter and sugar, stir constantly over medium heat until dates are soft and pulpy, about 5 minutes; remove from heat, beat until smooth, stand 5 minutes. Add remaining ingredients; mix thoroughly.

Spread evenly into greased and greased paper-lined 7 in. x 11 in. lamington tin. Top with Lemon Glacé Icing, refrigerate until set. Cut into bars.

Lemon Glace Icing: Sift 1½ cups icing sugar into heatproof basin, add 1 teaspoon butter and 2 tablespoons lemon juice, stir to combine. Stir constantly over simmering water until of spreading consistency.

Chocolate Almond Bars

8 oz. plain sweet biscuits	2 tablespoons brandy
2 oz. walnuts	1 teaspoon instant coffee powder
½ cup raisins	½ cup condensed milk
2 oz. glacé cherries	
2 oz. dark chocolate	

Almond Paste:

4 oz. ground almonds	1 egg
2½ cups icing sugar	2 teaspoons lemon juice

Crush biscuits finely; place in mixing bowl with very finely chopped walnuts, raisins and cherries; mix well. Melt chopped chocolate, add brandy, instant coffee and condensed milk; stir into dry ingredients, mix thoroughly. Press evenly into greased and lined 7 in. x 11 in. lamington tin. Refrigerate until firm.

Roll out Almond Paste, press on to chocolate base, smoothing surface with knife.

Top with Chocolate Topping, cover, and refrigerate overnight. Cut into small bars.

Almond Paste: In bowl combine sifted icing sugar and ground almonds; mix well. Stir in beaten egg and lemon juice. Place on surface dusted with icing sugar, knead until smooth.

Chocolate Topping: Chop 3 oz. dark chocolate roughly, place in top of double saucepan, with 1 oz. butter, stir over hot water until melted.

Special Occasion Biscuits

Chocolate Rum Sticks

6 oz. dark chocolate	4 oz. dark chocolate, extra
3 oz. unsalted butter	1½ oz. solid white
1 egg-yolk	vegetable shortening
2 teaspoons rum	

Melt chopped chocolate over hot water, allow to cool but not set. Cream butter until light and fluffy. Beat egg-yolk, gradually add creamed butter, about 1 tablespoon at a time, beat until just blended. When chocolate is cool, gradually blend it into the butter mixture, beat well. Refrigerate 5 minutes to stiffen slightly. Add rum, mix well.

Put mixture into piping bag fitted with ½ in. plain tube; pipe 2½ in. sticks on to waxed paper, freeze 20 minutes to firm.

Melt extra chocolate and shortening over hot water, cool; when beginning to thicken, coat sticks. Place on waxed paper, return to freezer for 10 minutes. Decorate with any remaining chocolate coating.

Makes 1½ to 2 dozen.

Brandied Chocolate Biscuits

4 oz. butter	⅓ cup ground rice
¼ cup castor sugar	pinch salt
1 cup plain flour	1 tablespoon brandy

Cream butter and sugar until light and fluffy. Add brandy, beat well. Gradually stir in sifted dry ingredients. Put into piping bag. Using fluted tube, pipe mixture into close zigzag or ring shapes about 2½ in. long or in diameter, on to lightly greased oven trays.

Bake in moderate oven 15 to 20 minutes or until light golden-brown. Loosen from tray while still hot; cool on wire rack.

When cold, dip top of biscuit in Chocolate Icing. Leave until set.

Chocolate Icing: Combine ½ oz. solid white vegetable shortening and 4 oz. chopped dark chocolate in top of double saucepan over hot water. Stir until melted and smooth.

Makes approx. 2 dozen.

Petit Fours

4 oz. butter	½ teaspoon vanilla
½ cup icing sugar	1⅔ cups plain flour
1 egg	glacé cherries

Cream together butter and sifted icing sugar until white and fluffy; add egg and vanilla, beat well. Stir in sifted flour. Fill mixture into forcing bag fitted with fluted tube. Pipe small amounts of mixture on to lightly greased oven trays; the biscuits should be small (approximately 1 in. in diameter).

Cut cherries into quarters, place a cherry quarter on top of each biscuit. Bake in moderately hot oven 7 minutes, until light yellow. Cool on trays.

Makes approx. 4 dozen.

Florentines

¾ cup sultanas	⅔ cup condensed milk
2 cups crushed cornflakes	3 oz. dark chocolate
3 oz. raw peanuts	
2 oz. chopped glacé cherries	

Combine all ingredients except chocolate in mixing bowl; mix well. Grease flat oven trays, line with greaseproof paper; grease paper, then dust lightly with cornflour. Shake trays to remove any excess cornflour.

Place dessertspoonfuls of mixture in small heaps on trays. Bake in moderate oven 15 to 20 minutes. Leave on trays to cool before lifting off carefully with spatula.

Melt chopped chocolate over hot water, remove from heat, and stir until thickened slightly. Spread chocolate over flat side of biscuit, mark with fork. Allow chocolate to set before storing in airtight tins.

Makes approx. 2½ dozen.

From back, Hazelnut Wafers, Petit Fours, Chocolate Hazelnut Biscuits and, in front, Chocolate Rum Sticks.

Rum Balls

9 oz. cake crumbs (approx. 3 cups)	2 tablespoons water
3 tablespoons apricot jam	2 tablespoons apricot jam, extra
3 tablespoons cocoa	chocolate sprinkles
1 tablespoon rum	

Warm apricot jam slightly, push through sieve.

Mix together cake crumbs, sifted cocoa, 3 tablespoons of jam, and rum until a stiff paste is formed. Make into approximately 2 dozen balls.

Heat extra jam with water, push through sieve; dip the balls in this jam mixture, then coat with chocolate sprinkles. Place in paper patty cases. Refrigerate until firm.

Chocolate Cherry Bars

6 oz. dark chocolate	2 cups coconut
3 eggs	4 oz. glacé cherries
1 cup castor sugar	icing sugar

Melt chocolate over hot water, beat until smooth. Spread evenly over base of greased 7 in. x 11 in. lamington tin with base lined with greased aluminium foil. Refrigerate until set.

Beat eggs lightly with fork, add sugar, beat until combined; fold in coconut and chopped cherries. Spread evenly over chocolate. Bake in moderate oven 30 minutes or until firm to touch. Cool, then refrigerate.

Before serving, sprinkle with sifted icing sugar, cut into small bars.

Golden Lace Biscuits

$\frac{1}{2}$ cup liquid glucose	1 cup plain flour
4 oz. butter	4 oz. finely chopped blanched almonds
$\frac{2}{3}$ cup brown sugar, firmly packed	

Combine glucose, butter and brown sugar in saucepan. Place over very low heat, stir until sugar dissolves, bring to boil, remove from heat immediately. Combine sifted flour and nuts, add to heated mixture, mix well together.

Drop by teaspoonfuls on to greased oven trays. Allow 2 biscuits to each tray, to allow for spreading.

Bake in moderate oven 5 to 6 minutes. Remove biscuits from oven, leave a few seconds to set slightly. Loosen with spatula; very quickly remove from oven trays. Place on wire rack to cool.

Delicious as accompaniment to desserts or ice-cream.

Makes approx. $4\frac{1}{2}$ dozen.

Hazelnut Truffles

1 cup icing sugar	$\frac{1}{4}$ cup cream
4 oz. ground hazelnuts	1 teaspoon rum
12 oz. dark chocolate	chocolate sprinkles
1 egg-white	

Sift icing sugar into bowl, mix with hazelnuts. Stir in just enough lightly beaten egg-white to make a firm paste; add cream.

Chop chocolate, place in top of double saucepan, stir over hot water until melted. Blend into hazelnut mixture, stirring with wooden spoon; add rum.

Turn mixture into shallow tin lined with greased greaseproof paper; refrigerate until set. When firm, cut into small squares, then roll into small balls between palms of hands; roll in sprinkles. Refrigerate.

Makes approx. $2\frac{1}{2}$ dozen.

Hazelnut Chocolate Squares

$1\frac{1}{4}$ cups self-raising flour	1 egg
pinch salt	$\frac{1}{2}$ teaspoon vanilla
$2\frac{1}{2}$ oz. butter	apricot jam
	4 oz. dark chocolate

Filling:

$3\frac{1}{2}$ oz. butter	$\frac{1}{2}$ teaspoon vanilla
$\frac{1}{3}$ cup sugar	8 oz. roasted hazelnuts, finely chopped
2 tablespoons water	

Sift flour and salt into basin, rub in butter, add beaten egg and vanilla, mix to a soft dough. Turn on to lightly floured board, knead lightly, roll to fit lightly greased 10 in. x 12 in. swiss roll tin.

Spread with a thin layer of warmed, sieved jam, top with filling. Bake in moderate oven 30 to 35 minutes. Cool slightly, cut into squares; when cold, dip half of each biscuit into melted chocolate.

Filling: Combine butter, sugar, water and vanilla in saucepan, stir over low heat until sugar is dissolved, increase heat, bring to boil; remove from heat, allow to become cold; add hazelnuts.

Note: If hazelnuts are unroasted when bought, it is easy enough to roast them at home; place nuts on baking tray, place in moderate oven for 15 to 20 minutes, or until lightly toasted. Remove from oven. Place nuts in clean cloth, rub vigorously to remove skins; chop nuts finely.

Coffee Creams

4 oz. butter	1 teaspoon instant
½ cup sugar	coffee powder
1 egg	1 tablespoon hot water
2 cups self-raising flour	

Coffee Butter Cream:

1 oz. butter	1 teaspoon instant coffee
½ cup icing sugar	powder
1 tablespoon full-cream	2 teaspoons hot water
milk powder	

Cream butter and sugar, add coffee dissolved in hot water, and egg. Beat well. Fold in sifted flour, mix thoroughly.

Place in piping bag with fluted tube, pipe on to greased oven trays. Bake in moderate oven, 10 to 12 minutes. Cool on tray.

When cold sandwich together with Coffee Butter Cream.

Coffee Butter Cream: Cream butter, add sifted icing sugar and powdered milk, beat well. Dissolve coffee in hot water, add to butter mixture, beat till smooth.

Makes 2 dozen complete biscuits.

Hazelnut Wafers

4 oz. butter	4 oz. ground hazelnuts
½ cup castor sugar	4 oz. dark chocolate
1 cup plain flour	½ oz. solid white vegetable
pinch salt	shortening

Cream butter and sugar until light and fluffy. Add sifted flour, salt, and ground hazelnuts; mix well. Turn out on to lightly floured surface; knead lightly. Roll out to 10 in. x 11 in. oblong. Cut into finger lengths ¾ in. x 1½ in., or into 1½ in. squares

Place on greased oven trays, bake in moderately slow oven 20 minutes or until firm but not brown. Allow to cool on trays.

Melt chopped chocolate and vegetable shortening over hot water; remove from heat. Dip half of each biscuit into chocolate mixture, place on aluminium foil to set. Keep biscuits refrigerated.

Makes approx. 6 dozen fingers or 3 dozen squares.

Brandy Snaps

2 tablespoons golden syrup	½ cup plain flour
2 oz. butter	2 teaspoons ground ginger
⅓ cup brown sugar,	pinch salt
firmly packed	

Place syrup, butter and brown sugar into saucepan, heat slowly until butter has melted, stirring occasionally. Sift flour, ginger and salt into a bowl, stir in syrup-and-butter mixture; mix well.

Drop dessertspoonfuls of mixture on to greased oven trays, allowing room for spreading. Bake in moderate oven 5 to 7 minutes, or until golden-brown. Remove from oven, cool 1 minute. With knife, lift brandy snap from tray. Roll immediately around the handle of a wooden spoon. Allow to firm and cool on spoon handle; remove. Just before serving, fill with whipped cream.

Makes 6 to 8 brandy snaps.

Note: Two brandy snaps will fit comfortably on to a baking tray. It is a good idea to bake only two at a time. If they firm up before you have time to mould them into shape, return to the oven for a few minutes to soften again.

Almond Bread ✓

3 egg-whites	4 oz. whole unblanched
½ cup castor sugar	almonds
1 cup plain flour	

Beat egg whites until soft peaks form, add sugar gradually, beat until dissolved. Fold in sifted flour and whole almonds. Spoon into lightly greased 8 in. x 4 in. loaf tin. Bake in moderate oven 30 to 40 minutes. Leave in tin until completely cold. Then remove from tin, wrap in aluminium foil, put aside for one or two days. Using very sharp knife, cut into wafer-thin slices. Place slices on oven trays, place in slow oven 45 minutes, or until completely dried out and crisp.

Serve just one slice with after dinner coffee. Or serve as a delightfully crisp biscuit with ice-cream.

Slices

Walnut Meringue Slice

Pastry:

4 oz. butter
⅔ cup sugar

½ teaspoon vanilla
1 cup plain flour

Topping:

2 egg-whites
⅔ cup sugar
1 teaspoon vanilla

8 oz. finely chopped
walnuts

Pastry: Beat butter, sugar and vanilla until light and fluffy. Add sifted flour, stir until combined. Press over base of greased 7 in. x 11 in. lamington tin, prick pastry well. Bake in moderate oven approximately 12 to 15 minutes; cool.

Topping: Beat egg-whites until soft peaks form, gradually add sugar, beating well. Stir in vanilla and walnuts; mix lightly. Spread over cold pastry base, bake in moderate oven 25 to 30 minutes or until meringue topping is firm. When cold, top with Chocolate Icing. (See recipe for Chocolate Slice, page 42).

Chocolate Walnut Slice

½ cup self-raising flour
pinch salt
1 cup rolled oats

½ cup brown sugar,
lightly packed
4 oz. butter

Filling:

2 oz. butter
2 oz. dark chocolate
⅓ cup sugar
1 egg
⅓ cup self-raising flour

⅓ cup plain flour
¼ cup milk
2 oz. chopped walnuts
½ teaspoon vanilla

Chocolate Icing:

½ oz. butter
1 oz. dark chocolate
¾ cup icing sugar

1 teaspoon vanilla
2 tablespoons hot water

Base: Sift flour and salt, place all dry ingredients into bowl. Add melted butter; mix well. Press mixture into greased 7 in. x 11 in. lamington tin, bake in moderate oven 10 minutes.

Pour filling over hot base, bake further 25 minutes. Remove from oven, stand 10 minutes, then top with Chocolate Icing. When the icing is set, cut into bars.

Filling: Melt butter and chopped chocolate over hot water; pour into mixing bowl. Add sugar and beaten egg, mix well. Add sifted flours alternately with milk, stir in vanilla and walnuts.

Chocolate Icing: Melt butter and chocolate over hot water, add sifted icing sugar, vanilla and water; beat until smooth.

Marshmallow Crunch

Base:

4 breakfast cereal
  biscuits
½ cup brown sugar,
  firmly packed
1 cup coconut

1 cup self-raising flour
½ teaspoon salt
5 oz. butter
3 tablespoons raspberry
  (or other) jam

Base: Crush biscuits and put in bowl. Add brown sugar, coconut, sifted flour, and salt. Melt butter and add to dry ingredients; mix well.

Press into well-greased 7 in. x 11 in. lamington tin. Bake in moderate oven 20 to 25 minutes or until base is firm; cool.

When base is cold, spread with jam, then quickly spread marshmallow over. When marshmallow is set, cut into squares with a knife dipped in hot water.

Marshmallow Topping: Put 1 cup sugar and 1 cup water into saucepan, sprinkle 1½ tablespoons gelatine over. Stir over heat until sugar is dissolved and mixture boils. Reduce heat, simmer 7 minutes, remove from heat. When mixture is nearly cold, add ½ teaspoon vanilla, beat until thick and fluffy.

Apple Slice

6 oz. butter
¾ cup sugar
2 eggs
1½ cups plain flour
1 teaspoon cinnamon

1 teaspoon mixed spice
1 lb. 13 oz. can
  unsweetened
  solid-pack pie apple
2 tablespoons sugar, extra

Beat butter until creamy, add sugar, then eggs one at a time, beating well after each addition. Stir in sifted flour and spices. Spread half the mixture over base of greased and greased paper-lined 7 in. x 11 in. lamington tin. Spread evenly with apple, sprinkle with extra sugar. Spread remaining cake mixture evenly over apple. Bake in moderate oven 50 minutes. Cool 10 minutes in tin, before turning on to wire rack to cool.

At back, Chocolate Rough Slice; on front tray, Malted Mocha Slice and, in front, Chocolate Walnut Slice. See pages 41, 44 and 38.

Coconut Slice

Pastry:

3 oz. butter	1¼ cups plain flour
¼ cup sugar	¼ cup self-raising flour
1 egg	

Topping:

2 egg-whites	3 cups coconut
1 cup sugar	raspberry jam
½ teaspoon vanilla	

Pastry: Beat butter until creamy, add sugar, beat until just combined. Add egg, beat well. Add sifted flours; mix well. Press into greased 9 in. slab tin; prick lightly. Refrigerate 15 minutes.

Topping: Beat egg-whites until soft peaks form, gradually add sugar; beat well after each addition. Stir in vanilla and coconut; mix well.

Spread a thin layer of raspberry jam over pastry. Spoon coconut mixture over, spread out evenly.

Bake in moderate oven 25 to 30 minutes or until coconut topping is light golden-brown. Allow to cool in tin.

Fruit Slice

4 oz. butter	2½ tablespoons cornflour
1½ cups self-raising flour	1 egg
⅓ cup ground rice	2 teaspoons castor
¼ cup castor sugar	sugar, extra

Filling:

½ lb. dates	2 oz. glacé cherries
2 teaspoons grated	1 oz. butter
lemon rind	1 teaspoon mixed spice
¼ cup lemon juice	¾ cup water
1 cup sultanas	1 tablespoon arrowroot
1 cup raisins	1 tablespoon rum or
1 oz. mixed peel	orange juice

Sift flour, ground rice and cornflour into basin, rub in butter until mixture resembles fine breadcrumbs. Stir in sugar and beaten egg. Knead lightly on floured board.

Roll out half pastry, fit into greased and lined 7 in. x 11 in. lamington tin. Cover with prepared filling. Roll out remaining pastry, cover filling. Brush with cold water, sprinkle extra sugar on top.

Bake in moderately hot oven 20 to 25 minutes, until lightly brown on top. Cool, cut into slices.

Filling: Place in saucepan chopped fruit and all ingredients except arrowroot and rum. Place over low heat, stir continually until thick. Blend arrowroot with rum or orange juice, stir into fruit mixture; return to heat; cook, stirring, until mixture boils and thickens. Cool completely.

Peanut Slice

Pastry:

2 oz. butter	2 tablespoons self-raising
2 tablespoons sugar	flour
1 egg	1 cup plain flour

Peanut Topping:

2 eggs, separated	1 tablespoon raspberry jam
¾ cup sugar	8 oz. roasted peanuts
1 oz. butter	(with skins on)
1 cup coconut	1 cup cornflakes

Pastry: Beat butter until creamy, add sugar, beat until combined. Add egg, beat well. Add sifted flours; mix well. Press into greased 7 in. x 11 in. lamington tin; prick pastry. Refrigerate 15 minutes.

Peanut Topping: Beat egg-yolks until creamy, add sugar, melted butter and raspberry jam; beat until thick and creamy. Stir in coconut and peanuts; mix well.

Beat egg-whites until soft peaks form, fold into peanut mixture with cornflakes. Spread over pastry, bake in moderate oven 30 to 35 minutes. Allow to cool in tin.

Chocolate Marzipan Slice ✓

3 oz. butter	¼ cup self-raising flour
2 tablespoons castor	2 teaspoons cornflour
sugar	pinch salt
¾ cup plain flour	½ teaspoon vanilla

Marzipan Filling:

4 oz. marzipan meal	⅓ cup castor sugar
1 tablespoon grated	1 small egg
lemon rind	

Cream butter and sugar, add vanilla and sifted dry ingredients, mix well. Press mixture over base of greased 7 in. x 11 in. lamington tin. Bake in moderate oven 15 minutes. Remove from oven immediately.

Spread evenly with Marzipan Filling. Return to oven, bake further 10 minutes. Cool, top with Chocolate Icing. Cut into fingers when set.

Filling: Combine marzipan meal, sugar and lemon rind. Add lightly beaten egg, mix well.

Chocolate Icing: Combine ½ oz. solid white vegetable shortening and 4 oz. chopped dark chocolate in top of double saucepan over hot water. Stir until melted and smooth.

Lemon Passionfruit Slice

Pastry:

1¼ cups self-raising flour	pinch salt
1¼ cups plain flour	1 teaspoon lemon juice
5 oz. butter	⅓ cup water, approx.

Filling:

2½ cups water	2 eggs
1¼ cups sugar	2 oz. butter
2 tablespoons grated lemon rind	⅓ cup lemon juice
⅓ cup cornflour	4 passionfruit
½ cup water, extra	milk
	extra sugar

Pastry: Sift flours and salt into bowl, rub in butter, mix to firm dough with lemon juice and water. Press together lightly.

Roll out two-thirds of pastry to fit base and up sides of lightly greased 7 in. x 11 in. lamington tin. Spread in filling, cover with remaining rolled-out pastry. Pinch edges of pastry lightly together. Brush top carefully with a little milk, sprinkle with a little extra sugar. Bake in moderate oven 40 minutes or until golden. Cool, then refrigerate until filling has set.

Filling: Put water, sugar and lemon rind in saucepan, bring to boil, stirring. Blend cornflour with extra water, stir into lemon mixture. Cook over heat until mixture boils and thickens, stirring constantly.

Remove from heat, add beaten eggs, butter, lemon juice and passionfruit pulp; blend well. Return to heat, simmer further 2 minutes, cool.

Vanilla Slice

1 lb. packaged puff pastry	2 pints milk
1 cup sugar	2 oz. butter
¾ cup cornflour	2 egg-yolks
½ cup custard powder	2 teaspoons vanilla

Passionfruit Icing:

1 cup icing sugar	1 passionfruit
1 teaspoon butter	1 teaspoon water, approx.

Have pastry at room temperature. Some 1 lb. packs of puff pastry come in two separate ½ lb. blocks; some come in one complete 1 lb. block. If using the former, roll each half separately, as below. If using the complete 1 lb. block, cut pastry in half.

Roll each half of pastry to a 13 in. square, then, with sharp knife, trim to 12 in. square.

Place one square of pastry on large ungreased oven tray, bake in very hot oven 5 to 10 minutes, or until well browned. Trim pastry with a sharp knife to 9 in. square.

Bake and trim remaining pastry in the same way. Flatten 'puffy' side of both pieces of pastry with hand.

Line a 9 in. square slab tin with aluminium foil, bringing the foil up over sides; this makes it easy to remove slice when set. Place one piece of pastry into base of tin, flattened side uppermost.

Combine sugar, cornflour and custard powder in heavy-based saucepan, mix well to combine. Blend with a little of the milk until smooth, stir in remaining milk; add butter. Stir mixture constantly over heat until custard boils and thickens, reduce heat, simmer 3 minutes. Remove from heat, quickly stir in vanilla, then stir in the beaten egg-yolks. Pour hot custard immediately over pastry in tin. Place remaining pastry on top of custard so the flattened side touches the hot custard. Press pastry firmly with hand. Spread evenly with Passionfruit Icing; when cool, refrigerate several hours, or overnight, until set.

Passionfruit Icing: Sift icing sugar into small basin, add softened butter and pulp from passionfruit. Add enough water, approximately 1 teaspoonful, to make icing of thick spreading consistency. (The amount of water needed will depend on size of passionfruit.) Beat well.

Chocolate-Rough Slice

Base:

4 oz. butter	1 cup self-raising flour
⅓ cup castor sugar	2 teaspoons cocoa
¼ cup coconut	pinch salt

Chocolate Rough Topping:

3 tablespoons condensed milk	1 oz. butter
1 tablespoon cocoa	1 cup coconut
1 cup sifted icing sugar	1 teaspoon vanilla

Base: Sift dry ingredients into basin, add sugar and coconut; stir in melted butter, mix well. Press into greased and greased paper-lined 7 in. x 11 in. lamington tin. Bake in moderate oven 25 minutes. Cool slightly on wire rack; cover with

Chocolate Rough Topping while still warm. Cut into slices when cold.

Chocolate Rough Topping: Combine all ingredients in basin, mix well.

Lemon Meringue Slice

Pastry:

4 oz. butter	1 cup plain flour
$\frac{1}{4}$ cup castor sugar	$\frac{3}{4}$ cup self-raising flour
$\frac{1}{2}$ teaspoon vanilla	$\frac{1}{4}$ cup custard powder
1 egg	

Filling:

1 cup sugar	3 egg-yolks
3 tablespoons cornflour	1 cup milk
1 tablespoon grated lemon rind	2 oz. butter
$\frac{1}{3}$ cup lemon juice	1 cup sour cream

Meringue:

3 egg-whites	$\frac{3}{4}$ cup castor sugar

Cream butter and sugar, add vanilla and egg; beat well. Sift flours and custard powder. Gradually add sifted dry ingredients to creamed mixture, mix well.

Roll pastry out on lightly floured surface, line base and sides of greased 7 in. x 11 in. lamington tin. Prick well with fork, refrigerate 30 minutes. Bake in moderately hot oven 15 to 20 minutes or until golden-brown. Cool in tin.

When cold, spoon in filling. Spread meringue over filling, taking it right to pastry edge, rough up lightly with fork. Bake in moderate oven 10 to 15 minutes or until meringue is set and pale golden-brown. Stand 1 hour, then refrigerate until set.

Filling: In saucepan combine sugar, cornflour, lemon rind and juice, egg-yolks, milk and butter. Stir over medium heat until mixture boils and thickens, reduce heat, cook 3 minutes. Allow filling to cool, then fold in sour cream.

Meringue: Beat egg-whites until soft peaks form, gradually add sugar, beating well after each addition until sugar is dissolved and mixture is of good meringue consistency.

Chocolate Slice

$1\frac{1}{4}$ cups self-raising flour	$2\frac{1}{2}$ oz. butter, softened
$\frac{3}{4}$ cup sugar	$\frac{1}{2}$ cup water
$\frac{1}{2}$ teaspoon bicarbonate of soda	$\frac{1}{2}$ teaspoon vanilla
$\frac{1}{3}$ cup cocoa	2 eggs

Peppermint Icing:

1 teaspoon oil	$\frac{1}{4}$ teaspoon peppermint essence
$2\frac{1}{4}$ cups icing sugar	
2 tablespoons milk	

Chocolate Icing:

3 oz. dark chocolate	$\frac{1}{3}$ cup water
1 teaspoon oil	2 cups icing sugar, approx.

Sift dry ingredients into small bowl of electric mixer. Add butter, water and vanilla. Beat on medium speed of electric mixer for 2 minutes. Add eggs, increase speed slightly, beat 2 minutes more.

Pour into greased 7 in. x 11 in. lamington tin. Bake in moderate oven 25 to 30 minutes. When cold, top with Peppermint Icing; allow this icing to set before spreading Chocolate Icing over.

Peppermint Icing: Put oil in basin, add sifted icing sugar and milk, mix to thick paste. Flavour to taste with peppermint essence. Put basin over simmering water, stir until icing is of smooth spreading consistency.

Chocolate Icing: Put chocolate, oil and water in top of double saucepan, stir until chocolate is melted; remove from heat. Gradually beat in sifted icing sugar; beat until smooth and of spreading consistency.

Currant Slice

Base:

1 cup plain flour	$\frac{3}{4}$ cup rolled oats
pinch salt	$\frac{1}{2}$ cup brown sugar, lightly packed
4 oz. butter	

Topping:

1 cup currants	1 cup water
$\frac{1}{2}$ cup sultanas	1 teaspoon grated lemon rind
1 tablespoon cornflour	1 tablespoon lemon juice
$\frac{1}{2}$ teaspoon cinnamon	

At back, delicious Fruit Slice; in front, Currant Slice, topped with pink icing. See pages 40 and 42.

Glace Icing:

¾ cup icing sugar   1 tablespoon milk
½ teaspoon butter   pink food colouring

Base: Sift flour and salt into basin, rub in butter, add oats and sugar. Press mixture evenly into greased 7 in. x 11 in. lamington tin. Top with topping, bake in moderate oven 35 minutes. Cool, drizzle with pink glacé icing. Cut into bars.

Topping: Wash currants and sultanas, combine in saucepan with cornflour, cinnamon and water; stir over medium heat until mixture boils and thickens. Add lemon rind and juice. Cool.

Glace Icing: Sift icing sugar into basin; add butter and milk, beat until smooth. Colour pale pink with few drops of food colouring. Stand icing over hot water, stir until of pouring consistency.

Jelly and Pineapple Slice

1 packet plain sponge   2 packets raspberry
    cake mix   jelly crystals
15 oz. can pineapple pieces   3 cups water

Make up sponge mix according to directions on packet. Pour half of mixture into greased and lined 7 in. x 11 in. lamington tin. Bake in moderate oven 25 minutes, or until cooked when tested. (Remainder can be baked in greased 6 in. square tin and used as cake). Remove from tin, allow to cool on wire rack.

When cold, return large cake to lamington tin, sprinkle with 2 tablespoons pineapple syrup. Cover with drained pineapple pieces.

Make up 2 packets of jelly using 3 cups boiling water; allow to set until of egg-white consistency. Carefully spoon over pineapple pieces. Refrigerate until set. Cut into slices.

Malted Mocha Slice

Base:

1 cup plain flour   ⅓ cup brown sugar
3 oz. butter   firmly packed

Topping:

2 tablespoons self-raising   2 eggs
    flour   1 teaspoon vanilla
½ cup malted milk   2 teaspoons drinking
    powder   chocolate
¼ cup sugar   2 oz. blanched almonds
pinch salt   ⅓ cup coconut

Malted Icing:

2 tablespoons malted-milk   1 oz. butter
    powder   2 teaspoons drinking
½ teaspoon instant coffee   chocolate
    powder   ½ teaspoon vanilla
1 tablespoon hot water   ¾ cup icing sugar

Base: Sift flour into bowl, rub in butter, add sugar, blend well. Press mixture over base of greased and greased paper-lined 8 in. square slab tin. Bake in moderate oven 15 minutes.

Topping: In mixing bowl combine flour, milk powder, sugar, salt, eggs, vanilla and chocolate; blend well. Stir in chopped almonds and coconut. Spread mixture over partially cooked base.

Bake further 25 minutes in moderate oven; cool. Spread with Malted Icing. Cut into slices.

Malted Icing: Combine milk powder, instant coffee and hot water; mix well. Add softened butter, chocolate, vanilla and sifted icing sugar. Beat well until smooth, adding a little more water, if necessary, to make a spreading consistency.

Apricot Cream Cheese Slice

Crumb Crust:

6 oz. plain sweet biscuits   3 oz. butter

Filling:

15 oz. can apricot   12 oz. packaged
    nectar   cream cheese
1 tablespoon gelatine   1 tablespoon lemon juice
½ cup castor sugar   ½ pint cream

Topping:

1 tablespoon arrowroot   2 teaspoons rum
1 tablespoon sugar

Crumb Crust: Crush biscuits finely, combine with melted butter, mix well. Press mixture firmly over base of 7 in. x 11 in. lamington tin, refrigerate.

Filling: Measure ¾ cup apricot nectar from can (reserve remainder for topping). Pour the ¾ cup nectar into saucepan, sprinkle gelatine over. Stir over low heat until gelatine is dissolved; allow to cool and thicken slightly.

Beat cream cheese and sugar until mixture is smooth and creamy, beat in lemon juice, then apricot mixture; fold in whipped cream. Pour on to crumb crust, refrigerate 2 hours or until firm.

Topping: Combine sugar and arrowroot in saucepan, blend in reserved apricot nectar. Stir constantly over heat until mixture boils and thickens. Remove from heat; add rum, continue stirring few minutes to cool slightly. Spread over cheese mixture, refrigerate 1 hour or until firm.

Index

Almond and Date Meringues   16
Almond Bread   37
Almond Crisps   12
Almond Fingers   22
Almond Macaroons   17
Almond Meringue Shortbread   20
Almond Rock Meringues   16
Amaretti   18
Anzac Biscuits   8
Apple Oatmeal Cookies   29
Apple Slice   38
Apricot and Nut Cookies   12
Apricot Bar Cookies   29
Apricot Cream Cheese Slice   44
Ayrshire Shortbread   22

Brandied Chocolate Biscuits   34
Brandy Snaps   37
Brown Sugar Meringues   16
Burnt Butter Biscuits   21
Butter Oat Biscuits   9

Caramel Cornflake Cookies   9
Cheese and Potato Biscuits   24
Cheese and Sesame Wafers   25
Cheese Biscuits   25
Cheese Blisters   24
Cheese Puffs   25
Cheese Straws   24
Cherry Tops   10
Chinese Chews   26
Choc-Mint Slices   33
Chocolate Almond Bars   33
Chocolate Biscuit Slice   32
Chocolate Cherry Bars   36
Chocolate Coconut Bars   10
Chocolate Crackles   32
Chocolate Cream Cookies   20
Chocolate Date Fingers   32
Chocolate Fruit Squares   32
Chocolate Fudge Shortbread   22
Chocolate Marzipan Slice   40
Chocolate Rough Slice   41
Chocolate Rum Sticks   34
Chocolate Slice   42
Chocolate Walnut Slice   38
Coconut Cheese Balls   25
Coconut Cookies   10
Coconut Crunch Biscuits   10
Coconut Fruit Fingers   6
Coconut Lemon Macaroons   17
Coconut Meringues   17
Coconut Oatmeal Cookies   18
Coconut Slice   40
Coffee Cream Meringues   16
Coffee Creams   37
Continental Almond Rounds   21
Continental Chocolate Slice   33
Cornflake Biscuits   8
Cornflake Chews   32

Cream Cheese Biscuits   24
Crisp Coconut Biscuits   10
Crispies   28
Crunchy Wholemeal Biscuits   28
Currant Cookies   6
Currant Fingers   21
Currant Slice   42
Curry Biscuits   25

Date and Walnut Cookies   6
Date and Walnut Slice   28

Easy Biscuits   8
Easy Coconut Macaroons   17

Flaky Cheese Biscuits   24
Florentines   34
French Butter Biscuits   30
Fruit Bars   29
Fruit Slice   40

Ginger Biscuits   13
Gingerbread Men   13
Ginger Currant Cookies   13
Ginger Nuts   13
Golden Lace Biscuits   36
Ground Rice Biscuits   18

Hazelnut Chocolate Squares   36
Hazelnut Macaroons   17
Hazelnut Truffles   36
Hazelnut Wafers   37
Honey Banana Biscuits   14
Honey Coconut Biscuits   14
Honey Ginger Snaps   14
Honey Jumbles   18
Honey Oat Biscuits   9
Honey Peanut Biscuits   29
Honey Sultana Cookies   14

Jam Drops   26
Jelly and Pineapple Slice   44

Lemon Cookies   9
Lemon Date Bars   33
Lemon Honey Drops   14
Lemon Meringue Slice   42
Lemon Passionfruit Slice   41
Lemon Shortbread Biscuits   6
Linzer Biscuits   30
Lunchbox Cookies   8

Malted Mocha Slice   44
Marshmallow Crunch   38
Melting Moments   26
Monte Carlos   26

Nutties   9

Oatmeal Crunchies   8

Oaty Crisps   8
One-Egg Meringues   17
Orange Coconut Cookies   10
Orange Honey Cookies   14

Paprika Biscuits   25
Passionfruit Slice   20
Peanut Butter Biscuits   12
Peanut Cookies   12
Peanut Crisps   12
Peanut Roughs   18
Peanut Slice   40
Petit Fours   34
Preserved Ginger Biscuits   13

Raisin Crunchies   28
Raspberry Almond Fingers   12
Raspberry Nougat Cookies   20
Rum Balls   36

Scotch Shortbread   22
Sesame Biscuits   21
Sesame Seed Fingers   29
Shortbread   22
Sour Cream Cookies   21
Sugar 'n' Spice Cookies   29
Sultana Coconut Cookies   20
Swiss Cakes   30

Vanilla Biscuits   6
Vanilla Slice   41
Viennese Biscuits   30

Walnut and Cheese Biscuits   24
Walnut Meringues   16
Walnut Meringue Slice   38
White Christmas   32
Wholemeal Date Slice   28
Wholemeal Oat Biscuits   9

Yo-Yo Biscuits   26